Gabbilam

Gabbilam

A DALIT EPIC

GURRAM JASHUVA

Translated from the Telugu by

CHINNAIAH JANGAM

YODA PRESS
79 Gulmohar Enclave
New Delhi 110 049
www.yodapress.co.in

ISBN: 9789382579366

Editors in charge: Tanya Singh and Arpita Das
Typeset by MSourcing
Published by Arpita Das for YODA PRESS

CONTENTS

To

Iti, Mayurika
and
Abhyuday

ACKNOWLEDGMENTS

A King died, and a star fell from the sky
A great poet died, and star went to heaven
King lived in a stone statue
And the poet lived on the tongues of people

–Gurrum Jashuva

Gabbilam's translation was an endeavor spanning decades of meditation along with a relentless struggle to understand the text's social, literary and historical context. Gurram Jashuva was the only Dalit poet I read in school as few stanzas from his writings were included in Telugu textbooks. While teaching, teachers always reminded us that Jashuva was a Madiga untouchable and still wrote excellent poetry. As a child, I did not understand the difficulty of becoming a writer, especially when one comes from a Dalit background. Given the Brahminical nature of Telugu curriculum, references to Jashuva faded away from the syllabus as I moved up in my studies. But his poems were sung on stage by Dalit artists like Bhandaru Rama Rao and others who dominated early-stage/drama performances. Plays such as *Satya Harishchandra* are performed across rural areas. The burial ground scene in which Jashuva's poems were recited became household lore. The rural masses repeated them in the fields and everyday affairs. As Jashuva himself wrote above, he became a people's poet.

When I joined the Center for Historical Studies in Jawaharlal Nehru University (JNU) in 1995 to pursue an MPhil, I intended to write a thesis on the development of national consciousness in Telugu country. I met Kancha Ilaiah, a fellow at the Nehru Memorial Museum and Library (Teen Murti). He used to visit the JNU campus often. One evening he asked about my research topic. His immediate reaction was, 'There will be many to write about privileged Savarnas, and why don't you research on Dalits?' He asked whether I was familiar with Dalit figures in Telugu, and I instantly mentioned Gurram Jashuva. He smiled and said, 'There you go, you found a topic and person to write about.' I expressed doubt whether I could write a thesis on a poet, and he replied with 'Why not?' I approached my research supervisor, K.N. Panikkar, and told him that I wanted to write my thesis on Jashuva. He agreed and encouraged me. From then on, my passion for engaging with Jashuva's writings remained steadfast and I often carried *Gabbilam* wherever I went.

However, it took me years to gather the courage to translate Jashuva's poems. On this journey, I acquired many debts. First and foremost is my wife, Mayurika Chakravorty. She listened to my translations and became my first cheerleader. Given her literary interests she began to appreciate the beauty of Telugu poetry and also began translating some Telugu poems of Vara Vara Rao and K.G. Satyamurti (Shiva Sagar).

Frances Montgomery generously read and edited the first draft of the translation and made it more accessible to the non-Telugu audience. She is my true well-wisher, and I cannot thank her enough for all the love and support. My lifelong friends, Sagari and Madhoo, remain a constant source of strength. They read multiple drafts and cross-checked poems with the Telugu original. They also suggested where I could place the illustrations in this book. They played a critical role in shaping this text, and I owe them a lot more than just thanks. I presented an early draft of the translation at the Telugu Studies conference organized by Lisa Mitchell at the University of Pennsylvania. I am very grateful for the invitation. Lisa and other participants at the conference, Daud Ali, Davesh Soneji, Afsar Muhammad, Rama Mantena, Ram Rawat, Chandra Mallampalli, Gautham Reddy, Srinivas Reddy, Jamal Jones, Subhashini Kaligotla and others, listened patiently, and I thank them all. Among them Gautham Reddy took keen interest in the translation and gave valuable suggestions in revising the introduction. He corrected many factual errors. He is very generous and shared his doctoral thesis that helped in contextualizing many aspects of the history of Telugu literature. I am very grateful for his time and passionate engagement with the text.

When I struggled to understand some poems, I accidentally mentioned them to Shashanka Mouli, an old college friend. He said that his father, Ashavadi Prakash Rao has done a verse rendering of *Gabbilam*. Reading verse rendering helped a lot in the completion of the project. I would like to thank Shashanka Mouli and his father who passed away recently. I often called Pillalamarri Ramulu to discuss about the social and literary intricacies of Telugu texts. I would like to thank him for his time and help.

While translating the text, I often thought about enriching its meaning and making it more accessible to non-Telugu audiences. To bring out *Gabbilam*'s intellectual rigor and engage with the readers, I thought about including illustrations that will captivate the audience and enhance the reading experience. When Arpita Das agreed with the idea, I approached three illustrators, Malavika Raj, Mansi Thapliyal and Ale Laxman. All of them generously submitted illustrations within a short deadline. The editorial team had a difficult choice and the final selection wasn't easy. I would like to thank Malavika and Mansi for submitting the illustrations. I would like to thank Avinash Kumar for introducing Mansi to me. I am fortunate to get an opportunity to work with Laxman Ale, a renowned illustrator and painter from Telangana. K. Satyanarayana introduced us and he made this project of illustrations his own. His drawings are marvelous and meaningful, capturing and representing Jashuva's emotions. Thus, I would like to thank K. Satyanarayana and Laxman for being fellow travelers. When I wanted to apply for funding for these illustrations, I approached James Miller, Chair of the History Department, Carleton University. He introduced me to Carol Payne, Associate Dean, Research and International at the Dean's Office, Faculty of Arts and Social Sciences, Carleton University. She encouraged me to apply for an SSHRC Knowledge Mobilization Grant through the Carleton Office of Research Initiatives and Services (CORIS). I would thank James Miller, Carol Payne and Sarah Adams for helping with a grant application to support illustrations.

In one of my research trips to Montreal, I discovered a copy of *Gabbilam* translated by Raja Rao in 1973 at the McGill University library. Kaki Madhava Rao also translated *Gabbilam* in 1996. Both were retired Indian Administrative Service (IAS) officers and hail from the Dalit community. While adding academic perspective, my translation places *Gabbilam* in its historical and literary context. I would like to thank Kaki Madhava Rao for sending his translated copy of *Gabbilam*. In compiling a bibliography of Jashuva's writings and writings on Jashuva in Telugu, I would like to thank Ginnarapu Aadi Narayana for going to different libraries and the Hyderabad Book Fair to get information about the latest writings on Jashuva.

In completing this project, my colleagues at the Carleton University Academic Staff Association (CUASA), especially the Grievance Committee members, generously relieved me from the burden of committee work. I would like to thank Angelo Mingarelli, Christal Cote, Hanan Mankal and Alex Aucoin. My dearest colleagues Audra Diptee and Alek Bennett have always been a source of strength and encouragement. I would like to thank them from the bottom of my heart. Sudipto Kaviraj, a teacher and mentor, inspired and encouraged me to engage with Telugu language and literature. I am very grateful to him. I lost three teachers in the last two years, Sheik Mannan, Rai Rama Rao and N.S.N. Reddy. All of them played a critical role in my endeavor to pursue higher studies. I remember them with gratitude for helping me reach this stage in life.

This book would not have materialized without Arpita Das. She has been equally passionate about the project from day one. I would like to thank Gita Ramaswamy for asking me to write to Arpita. Gita also reached out to MaNaSu Foundation which owns the copyright to Jashuva's writings to grant translation permission to me. I would like to acknowledge the generosity of the MaNaSu Foundation and thank them as well. Working with Tanya Singh was a pleasant experience, and she patiently edited the text and suggested changes. In fact, she molded the voice of the text. Finally, I would like to thank Arpita, Tanya and the Yoda Press team for all the help in publishing the book. Harshavardhan Rao Pilli and Vijay Puli who were fellow travellers in intellectual pursuits and anti-caste activism. I would like to express my Jai Bhim to them. Finally, I would like to thank the journal *Indian Economic and Social History Review* for the permission to use my previously published article on Jashuva in writing the introduction.

My son Abhyuday Jangam, mother-in-law Iti Chakraborty and wife Mayurika Chakravorty provided the much-needed love and strength. They helped in finishing the book with delicious meals, chai and support. I dedicate this book to the three of them for being the source of my emotional and intellectual strength.

TRANSLATOR'S NOTE

In a foreword to his classic novel *Kanthapura*, Raja Rao writes about the problem of translation as

> The telling has not been easy. One has to convey in a
> language that is not one's own; the spirit is one's own.
> One has to convey the various shades and omissions
> of a certain thought movement that looks maltreated
> in an alien language. I use the word "alien", yes English
> is not really an alien language to us. It is the language
> of our intellectual make-up, like Sanskrit or Persian
> was before, but not of our emotional make-up.[1]

Similarly, I struggled to translate *Gabbilam*, a book of poetry that uses classical Telugu, Sanskrit and brings words from the spoken language of everyday life experiences of rural folk. Since Telugu is my mother tongue and I was educated in a Telugu medium school till my undergraduate studies, I made every effort to translate the original meaning of the words and sentences. I tried to be as truthful to the emotional expression of the poetry as possible. Jashuva followed classical poetic meter—not to succumb to the traditional Brahminical etiquette but to challenge and transform. Thus, every poem has a deep philosophical meaning that is incomparable. Sometimes that original emotion gets lost in translation, and the only way to do justice is to be as honest and transparent as possible to make the reader feel the pulse of Jashuva's work.

All translations are mine, and I did not use any words or sentences from previous translations of others. I have used and translated names of cities and towns, sometimes current names and other times used the old names, as per the original. I did not use diacritical marks and instead transliterated phonetically, the way words are pronounced in Telugu and Sanskrit.

---

1 Raja Rao, *Kanthapura*, Oxford University Press, New Delhi, 2009 (originally published in 1938).

INTRODUCTION

Gurram Jashuva in Social and Historical Context

Denial of education to oppressed sections of society, especially Dalits, is fundamental to perpetuating the caste system and its ideology. Brahminism, as a ruling ideology, elevated learning and knowledge as the exclusive, elitist enterprise of Brahmins for centuries, making writing and reading an alien experience for Dalits and other oppressed sections of society. In that historical backdrop, Dalit acquaintance with education is hardly a hundred years old. Following their own political and civilizing agendas, the colonial state and the Christian missionaries opened special schools for Dalit children. This unintended consequence of the colonial encounter made Dalits use educational opportunities as a way to escape from caste oppression and Brahminical domination. In this way the colonial education as a non-Brahminical tool, imbued with ideas of enlightenment, ignited the anti-caste thought that, till then, existed in folk tales, cultural performances and acts of defiance as everyday forms of resistance.[2] To trace the historical and intellectual roots of Gurram Jashuva's writings, one needs to go beyond the colonial period and Hindu Brahminical literary traditions. The anti-caste non-Brahminical oral tradition survived as a subversive tactic and sometimes as a direct challenge to the dominant ideology in non-literary forms. Honing these resistant histories of Dalit and Bahujan people is vital to understanding the writings of intellectuals like Jashuva.

The dominant writings in the Indian subcontinent, both historical and literary, source their arguments about the precolonial era and English archival tradition in the colonial period based on Sanskritic Brahminical

---

2 James C. Scott in his *Weapons of the Weak: Everyday Forms of Peasant Resistance*, Yale University Press, New Heaven, 1985, writes about the constant struggle between oppression and resistance in which peasants use Brechtian modes of resistance as a tactic of survival and to dodge oppression. Similarly, Dalits and other lower castes used music, songs, folk festivals and performances to resist oppression and subvert Brahminical hegemony.

tradition, or the Persian/Urdu tradition, in the postcolonial era. Even in regional languages like Telugu, the textual production was monopolized by Brahmins as they guarded the intellectual milieu to conform to caste ideology even if non-Brahmins wrote it. Thus, the discursive power in the Indian subcontinent was geared towards normalizing the Brahminical perspective. The world represented through the prism of Brahminism became a norm, and the oppressed and marginalized do not figure in that framework. From the Brahminical perspective, caste exists as a matter of fact. It does not cause any moral discomfort and makes them conscious of their inherited caste privileges. To break into such a guarded fortress of the literary sphere is an incredible adventure for a person from the lower caste of untouchables. One must scale against the caste-based systemic structural impediments that push down at every step of the way. At the same time, resisting structural barriers, very few from lower castes could withstand and prove themselves as equals to Brahminical elites in literary creativity and intellectual articulations.

The making of Gurram Jashuva as a poet and anti-caste visionary is part of an oral and cultural tradition that challenged caste inequality and oppressive Brahminical practices for centuries. That history precedes colonialism and exists as an alternative memory and consciousness to withstand caste-based oppression and dehumanization. To recuperate that anti-caste epistemology, one must abandon the colonial state constructed territorial and linguistic frames.[3] In the pre-colonial landscape, oral traditions, folk performances, social satire and caste *Puranas* were not part of the elite linguistic or territorial templates that the rulers patronized.[4] They trespassed all the customary covenants and traveled across regions, languages and cultures. The masses moved and strengthened their castes and

---

3 Gramophone recordings, collected across South Asia during 1913–29 as part of the Linguistic Survey of India, discovered Telugu language speakers beyond the borders of present Telugu states in places like Nagpur. These fascinating recordings reveal the way the colonial/modern idea of linguistic states is itself a construction and not natural. For further reading visit: https://dsal.uchicago.edu/books/lsi/about-lsi.html

4 Michel de Certeau in his *The Practice of Everyday Life*, California University Press, 2011, analyses and presents the ways in which the masses (popular) 'evade and manipulate' repressive mechanisms of discipline and establish a counter to domination. In this way survival and cultural practices of the lower castes weave multiple mechanisms to resist and survive Brahminical power and ideology.

communities, subverting the power of dominant Brahminical elites, Brahmin pandits and their patrons, i.e., rulers.

Gurram Jashuva was born in Vinukonda village in the Guntur district of Andhra Pradesh on 28 September 1895. Before colonial conquest, especially in the ancient and medieval periods, the Palnadu region where the village is situated stood on a crossroads, connecting different regions like modern-day Rayalaseema, Telangana, Karnataka, Tamil Nadu and Orissa, and acted as the gateway to the Coromandel coast that connected to the Indian Ocean trade networks.[5] After the decline of the Mauryan empire, the Satavahanas ruled this region in ancient times. Non-Brahminical religions like Jainism and Buddhism flourished, which enabled a vibrant agricultural and trading economy. They also had a liberal attitude towards social intercourse between different castes and did not patronize elaborate Brahminical sacrificial rituals.[6] After the slow decline of the Satavahanas, Brahminism emerged as a counter-revolution. It established itself as the ruling ideology in the medieval period.[7]

The resistance to Brahminical oppression and articulation of egalitarian traditions that continued throughout history in the Deccan Palnadu played an important role. The historic battle of Palnadu in the twelfth century, along with the family feud, was also a rivalry between rigid Brahminism and egalitarian aspirations. The main spark for the battle of Palnadu was the minister and military general Brahmanaidu's decision to open the gates of the Chennakesava temple to people of all castes; his opponents used this as a ruse to unseat him.[8] Gurram Jashuva was proud of his origins and that he was born into this geographical region's legacy of anti-Brahminism. He paid tribute to the region's history, especially its tumultuous social and religious conflicts that challenged the Brahminical status quo.

5 P. Swarnalatha, *The World of the Weaver in Northern Coromandel 1750–1850*, Orient Blackswan, Hyderabad, 2005. This book provides the social history of the production of cotton textiles that became a global commodity in the Indian Ocean trade networks.

6 Himanshu Prabha Ray, Trade in the Western Deccan under the Satavahanas, *Studies in History*, Vol. I, No.1, pp. 15–35.

7 Cynthia Talbot. *Precolonial India in Practice: Society, Region and Identity in Medieval Andhra*, Oxford University Press, 2001.

8 Gene Henry Roghair, *The Epic of Palnadu: A Study and Translation of Palnati Virula Katha, A Telugu Oral Tradition from Andhra Pradesh, India*, Clarendon Press, London, 1982.

Moreover, the social context of Jashuva's origins was another dimension to locate him in a larger anti-caste tradition. His father, Veeraiah, belonged to a touchable caste called Golla,[9] and his mother, Lingamamba, was an untouchable Madiga. They met at the American Baptist Mission school, fell in love and got married, breaking caste barriers as converted Christians. In this regard, the American Baptist Mission establishing its social base among the untouchable Madigas, itself, was a fascinating episode in the history of anti-caste politics. In 1805, British and Canadian Baptist missions started proselytizing activities in Telugu-speaking areas. They miserably failed to convert caste Hindus into Christianity. Then they handed over the mission to the newly arrived American missionary John E. Clough. While documenting the history of the mission, Clough and his wife Emma Rauschenbusch-Clough describe how Madiga untouchables adopted Christianity.

Even before the arrival of European missionaries, Madigas were engaged in the anti-caste movement as Bandiktla Veeramma followers. Veeramma, a female saint, preached social equality and was the follower of a seventeenth-century anti-caste saint, Potuluri Veerabrahmam. He was famous for his *kalagnanam* (prediction of the future).[10] He initiated Veeramma into his anti-caste egalitarian mission. Veeramma's follower Yerraguntla Peraiah was also the first Madiga to convert to Christianity and led the Madiga movement against caste discrimination and the practice of untouchability by introducing them to the American Baptist Mission. According to Clough, the American Baptist Mission's egalitarian philosophy of Christianity was spread using the well-established anti-caste network of Madigas in villages across Palnadu and Rayalaseema.

---

9 Golla is a lower caste in Andhra Pradesh and Telangana and in caste hierarchy they are Shudra, hence a touchable caste. For more details see Thurston and Rangachari, *Castes and Tribes of Southern India,* Government Press, Madras, 1909, pp. 284–96. According to them the social status of Golla is fairly high as they are allowed to mix freely with the Kapu, Kamma, Balija and other Shudra castes. Brahmins will even take buttermilk from their hands. The hereditary occupation of Gollas is to tend to sheep, cattle and sell milk (pp. 184–85).

10 Stephen Fuchs, an Austrian anthropologist, in his *Rebellious Prophets: A Study of Messianic Movements in Indian Religions,* Asia Publishing House, 1965 writes about Veerabrahmam and the social base of his movement among Madigas. In fact, the chapter is titled 'Among the Madigas.'

Interestingly these regions were part of the Virashaiva movement that blazed across modern-day Karnataka and Telangana as an anti-Brahmin movement.[11] They were part of the Satavahana empire that nurtured anti-caste and anti-Brahminical traditions in the ancient period. The Brahminical counter-revolution assimilated anti-caste traditions and annihilated anti-caste alternative visions of Jain and Buddhist thinkers. However, these philosophies continued as popular folk and oral traditions of lower castes in society. Brahminical reconstruction of history erased those traditions and presented Brahminization or Aryanization of Deccan and South India as the dawn of history.[12] Thus Jashuva's geographical location and social context are deeply embedded in the Protestant tradition that challenged Brahminism and social inequality. In this way, Jashuva's parents' inter-caste marriage was part of the larger thread of anti-caste history. His parents paid a heavy price for their revolt as they were ostracized by their respective castes, which instilled in him a spirit of anti-caste consciousness within him.

Poetics of Caste

There is a genesis story about the first Telugu poet Nannaya Bhattu a Brahmin from the eleventh century. According to the legend, the Chalukya king Raja Raja Narendra in the eleventh century asked scholars to translate the Sanskrit *Mahabharata* into the language of his subjects, i.e., Telugu. He claimed lineage from the Pandavas even though the early Chalukyas were Jain. This gesture indicates the gradual transition of ruling elites into the fold of Brahminism. Before Nannaya completed his translation, Atharvana, a Jain scholar finished a Telugu version of *Mahabharata* and showed it to Nannaya; the latter saw the superior composition of Atharvana and felt his version of *Mahabharata* would be turned down by the king. So, Nannaya set fire to the house of Atharvana and burnt the manuscript. Agonized, Atharvana cursed Nannaya who became a lunatic. That left the translation

---

11 Jan Peter Schouten, *Revolution of the Mystics: On the Social Aspects of Virasaivism,* Motilal Banarsidass, Delhi, 1995.

12 See K. A. Nilakanta Sastri's *A History of South India: From Prehistoric Times to the Fall of Vijayanagar,* Oxford University Press, Madras,1958. This is a classic text that presents the history of South India from the Brahminical perspective.

of the *Mahabharata* incomplete for three centuries as Nannaya had only finished three cantos out of the eighteen.

This story can be interpreted in two ways. First, historically, Telugu literature and language preceded Nannaya and calling him the originator of Telugu language and literature itself is a Brahminical conspiracy. No language development can be attributed to a single individual, and literary and spoken language is a collective social experience and contribution. Moreover, Deccan was the heartland of the Satavahana empire where Buddhism and Jainism flourished, and the early preceptors of Telugu probably were Jains and Buddhists. Second, the resurgence of Telugu language and literature closely aligned with Brahminical reaction against the existing Jain and Buddhist tradition in the name of the Vaidiki movement. The Vaidiki movement was a reactionary revivalist movement spearheaded by Brahmins reshaped religion, political institutions, and literature across centuries to naturalize caste *dharma* and Brahminical supremacy. From the eleventh century onwards, five centuries were spent translating the Sanskrit *Mahabharata*, *Ramayana,* and other Brahminical *Puranas* into Telugu to reaffirm the Brahminical vision and make it the ruling ideology of the state. In their pioneering history of Telugu literature, P. Chenchiah and Raja M. Bhujanga Rao said 'the impulse for translation had its origin in the revival of Brahmanism and the zeal to spread Vaidiki movement. This religious movement had the support of kings, the approbation of the literati, and above all, the sympathy of people. The long-drawn struggle between Jainism and Hinduism had ended in the victory of Brahmanism.'[13] In his pioneering studies, B. R. Ambedkar pointed out the continuous struggle in Indian history between the anti-caste egalitarian traditions like Jainism and Buddhism and their nemesis Brahminism; the history of Telugu literature further affirms his analysis.[14] The troubling origins of the Telugu language and literature are erased in mainstream scholarship. For example, Bhadriraju Krishnamurti, a linguist, traced the common origin of Kannada and Telugu languages in the sixth century. After the fifteenth century, the Telugu script diverged and developed into

---

13 P. Chenchiah and Raja M. Bhujanga Rao, *A History of Telugu Literature*, Oxford University Press, Madras, 1928, p. 41.

14 B. R. Ambedkar, Revolution and Counter Revolution in Vasant Moon (compiled), *Dr. B.R. Ambedkar Writings and Speeches*, Vol. 3, Government of Maharashtra, 1987.

independent languages.[15]Nevertheless, he had nothing to say about the violent origins of the language and Brahminical revivalism.

In this way, for centuries, the main content and meaning of literature in Telugu centered on the translation of epics, *Mahabharata* and *Ramayana*. People were scared to continue the translation fearing the curse of Nannaya and the completion of translation of the Mahabharata took another two hundred years. The secular and non-religious literature was the secondary by-product of that primary mission. Moreover, anti-Brahminical literature and movements were suppressed and persecuted by the rulers at the behest of Brahmin priests. That is why Cattamanchi Ramalinga Reddy wrote 'the ruthless manner in which the Buddhist and Jain literature in Sanskrit as well as the vernaculars, was suppressed and destroyed through the Brahminical reaction is the greatest tragedy of Indian culture…. The real motive underlying the translation of Mahabharata into Telugu with all its pro-Brahminical interpolations was propaganda through the vernaculars, as a counterblast to the Buddhist and Jain propaganda.'[16]

The break from that monotonous translation tradition occurred in the early modern era under Krishnadevaraya, the ruler of the Vijayanagar empire. Krishnadevaraya came from 'low-caste humble origins'[17] and emerged as an illustrious ruler of his time and an accomplished scholar in Sanskrit, Kannada and Telugu. His period, identified as the golden age, inaugurated a new epoch in Telugu literature known as the Prabandha or Kavya period.[18] Historically, it was a significant shift from the earlier periods. Unlike the obsession with the translation of the Sanskrit *Mahabharata*, *Ramayana*, and *Bhagavatam*, Prabandhas or Kavyas took episodes from

---

15 Bhadriraju Krishnamurti, *The Dravidian Languages*, Cambridge University Press, Cambridge, 2003, pp. 78–79.

16 P. Chenchiah and Raja M. Bhujanga Rao, *A History of Telugu Literature*, Oxford University Press, Madras, 1928, p. 41.

17 Srinivas Reddy, *Raya: Krishnadevaraya of Vijayanagara*, Juggernaut, New Delhi, 2020.

18 'The etymological meaning of the term Prabandha is that which is closely bonded. Telugu Prabandhas refer to a type of narrative in which a single storyline revolves around a noble and virtuous hero. Use of eighteen types of description, use of sringara or veera rasa and unity of emotion are some of the salient features of a prabandha.' C. Vijayasree, 'The Birth of a Genre: Telugu Novel in the Nineteenth Century' in Meenakshi Mukherjee (ed.), *Early Novels in India*, Sahitya Akademi, New Delhi, 2002, p.105.

the *Puranas* as a subject, and self-expression became central to poetry. The crowded epic narratives were replaced with an imaginative description of individuals' episodes and heroic lives and deeds. Even though the main themes were centered on religion and divine figures, semi-divine figures like Shankaracharya and Ramanuja emerged as heroes in some Kavyas. However, the political eclipse of the Vijayanagar empire in the sixteenth century was a blow to the literary grandeur of Telugu as royal patronage was lost with it. The Nayaka kingdoms that emerged from the ruins of the Vijayanagar empire like Thanjavur, Madurai, Pudukottai and Mysore supported Telugu poets.

Colonialism and Modernization of Telugu Language and Literature

After the decline of the Vijayanagar empire, even though there was no sustained patronage for Telugu, the Nayaka kingdoms and other royal families patronized Telugu scholars as a way to legitimize their power, enabling Telugu literature to flourish in diverse and creative ways. The nineteenth century introduction of the East India Company's rule and the consolidation of the colonial power was predicated on the assimilation of Brahmins and the Brahminical elites into the colonial institutional structures at various levels. The orientalists aka Madras School of Orientalists played a crucial role in the revival of classical Telugu in collaboration with the Brahmins. The East India Company officials and the colonial state officials, in their efforts to modernize education, recruited Brahmin pandits to produce language material and pedagogical tools that valorized a Sanskritized version of Telugu. Even the Christian missionaries followed their methods. In this endeavor printing press acted as an important medium to mass produce a variety of texts that enabled the emergence of an upper caste educated middle class as a distinct public.[19] In this way, as Sudipta Kaviraj succinctly argued, the project of modernity in the colonial period was 'state-centric' and had 'selective me-

19 Gautham Reddy in his unpublished doctoral thesis An Empire of Literary Telugu: Remaking Language and Community in Colonial South India 1812–1920 provides a detailed historical account of reproduction of classical (Brahminical) Telugu to suit the colonial modern educational needs.

diation' with indigenous institutions.[20] Telugu language's transformation under colonial influences is a perfect example of multiple applications of modernity and its reception. Also significantly, the colonial state and missionaries propelled modernization of the language, which was earlier appropriated by caste Hindu elites, particularly Brahmins who used it for social and religious reforms, political education and modernization of the upper echelons of society. The colonial missionaries' translations of the *Bible* into Telugu and publication of *Psalms* for conversion and church gatherings went hand in hand with the creation of Telugu textbooks and dictionaries for colonial officials, emphasizing prose. The usage of *gramya,* the language understood by the unlettered masses, increased as they contributed a lion's share to the colonial exchequer.[21] In the endeavor to modernize the Telugu language, the printing press proved vital too. The first step in this direction was the compilation of Telugu dictionaries by William Brown in 1807 and A. D. Campbell in 1810. Afterwards, Charles Philip Brown took it further and published Telugu English and English Telugu dictionaries during 1852–54 that helped language standardization.[22] As a civil servant, Brown had heard the verses of Vemana from the ordinary people in his field visits and collected and translated them into English in 1829.

The colonial state-led modernization process of the Telugu language had contradictory outcomes. At one level, the colonial state, through its investment in reviving classical or pre-modern Telugu, empowered Brahmins to have control over modern education. On the other hand, by providing access to education to non-elite and oppressed sections of society they threatened to loosen the grip of Brahmins and their upper caste patrons over archaic language and classical traditions centered on the poetic form. In this way schools established

---

20 Sudipta Kaviraj, Modernity and Politics in India in Shamuel N. Eisenstadt (ed.), *Multiple Modernities*, Routledge, 2002, pp. 137–62.

21 J. Mangamma in her book *The Rate Schools of Godavari,* Government of Andhra Pradesh, 1973, pointed out that non-Brahmin peasants paid extra tax for opening new schools in villages in Godavari districts.

22 Gidugu Venkata Sitapati wrote an essay tracing the history of dictionary writing in Europe and India, including in the Telugu language. 'Nighantu Rachana Parinamamu (Evolution of Dictionary Writing)' in William Brown, *Telugu English Nighantuvu,* Cultural Books Limited, Madras, 1953 (first published in 1818), pp. 1–6.

by the colonial state and the curricular development became a battle-ground for recasting Brahminical hegemony in the guise of 'High Telu-gu' that is overtly Sanskritized. Thus, institutions like Fort St. George and Madras University High School reproduced the Telugu classical language as a *granthika bhasha* away from the *gramya*, the everyday language of the people. For example, Paravastu Chinnaya Suri, a Telugu pandit under the service of East India Company rule, tried to enforce an archaic language for prose and his *Balavyakaranam*, a text on the Telugu grammar, set the standard.[23] While keeping tight control over the production of the language material and dissemination of literature, they used clandestine means to ensure Brahminical monopoly. When C. P. Brown published the verses of Vemana in English translation, they protested the anti-Brahminical satire. They forced the college board to stop sales and circulation. It took ten years for Brown to know that his book was being suppressed and he later secured an order for its circu-lation.[24] Nearly two hundred years of colonial state initiatives and mis-sionary activities led to aspirational elites' growth from the upper ech-elons of society influenced by European modernity. In Telugu country, English educated and westernized Brahmin elites like Kandukuri Vee-resalingam Pantulu,[25] Gurajada Appa Rao, and Gidugu Venkata Rama-murti[26] embraced the project of language modernization and used it as a tool to advocate social reforms such as widow remarriage, women's education, ban on bride price and child marriages. They wrote novels, plays, autobiographies, histories in modern prose. They selectively used the project of colonial modernity to modernize caste Hindu families, raise awareness about political modernity, and prepared the ground for nationalist consciousness. However, as the social reformer N. G. Chan-

---

23 Gautham Reddy's thesis elaborately discusses the role of Chinnaya Suri in the stan-dardization of Telugu in a medieval Sanskrit orientation as a classical language. Moreover, he also points out that Chinnaya Suri was a rare non-Brahmin from the Satani Srivaishnava caste to reach such heights in scholarship, leading Brahmins to question his scholarly au-thenticity.

24 G. V. Sitapati, *History of Telugu Literature*, Sahitya Akademi, New Delhi, 1968, p.108.

25 Vakulabharanam Rajagopal, Fashioning Modernity in Telugu: Viresalingam and his Interventionanist Strategy, *Studies in History*, Vol. 21, No.1, 2005, pp. 44–77.

26 Rama Sundari Mantena, Vernacular Publics and Political Modernity: Language and Prog-ress in Colonial South India, *Modern Asian Studies*, Vol. 47, No. 5, 2013, pp. 1678–1705.

davarkar rightly said, 'the customs and institutions with which the so-cial reformer propose to deal are common to the higher classes of the Hindu society ... they had almost no meaning for lower-caste groups at the time they were undertaken.'[27]

Nevertheless, the colonial state-backed modern prose won in the tussle between classical tradition tied to archaic language versus modern prose. It facilitated the spread of education among all castes and communi-ties, including untouchable Dalits. Education combined with print culture became a tool of emancipation to articulate anti-Brahmin consciousness through newspapers, journals, novels, and petitioning. Even though the colonial state did not patronize classical traditionalists, they used innova-tive methods to retain their hegemonic hold on language and literature. They perpetuated the supremacy of archaic language and poetic form through *Ashtavadam*, *Satavadhanam*, and *Jantakavulu* as superior liter-ary achievements.[28] In their endeavor, the old royal families of Pithapuram,

---

27 N. G. Chandavarkar, *The Speeches and Writings of the Honorable Justice Sir N. G. Chadavarkar*, The Manoranjak Grantha Prasarak Mandali, Bombay, 1911, p. 54.

28 Avadhanams (Ashtavadhanam and Satavadhanam) is a special aspect of the Telugu poets. Ashtavadhanam means the performance of eight feats of intellectual importance during the same period of time. Eight scholars sit around the Ashtavadhani, each with an item assigned to him to engage with the performer; one would ask him to compose a verse with a particular theme in a particular meter; another would request him to compose a verse avoiding the letters of the alphabet which he (the proposer) bans; another engages the per-former in a desultory conversation; another engages him in a game of chess; another strikes a bell now and then, and the performer should tell the total number of strokes at the end; an-other shows him a slip on which a single syllabic letter of a verse or sentence is written along with its serial number. These slips are shown now and then in an irregular order during the performance, and the performer has to give the complete verse or sentence in its regular or-der at the end. Satavadhanam means the composition of one hundred verses at a stretch in a conventional order. One hundred persons sit in the hall, each with a suggestion regarding the theme and the meter. The performer has to dictate the first lines of the hundred verses, one after another, to each of the hundred persons assembled. Then, the second lines are dictated by the performer, recollecting without any help from the audience, the first line he had dictated. This is a tedious task for both the performer and the audience, and to reduce the tediousness a convention has developed according to which the audience should be satisfied with thirty or forty verses and the performer may dictate the first two lines on one day and the remaining two lines the next day. The performer has to depend entirely on his memory, and is not expected to get any help in recollecting the theme or meter or the lines which he had previously dictated. He should not note anything on paper. Madabhushi Ven-

Nuzividu, and Vizianagaram played a critical role through patronage and hosting events to elevate classical poetry. Thus, writing in classical archaic language and poetic form was kept on a high pedestal even by modern scholars.

Moreover, using the ordinary folk language *gramya* in writing is viewed with contempt and equated with vulgarity. Therefore, budding poets had to swim in the ocean of classical tradition and write in a poetic form to command respect and get recognition. Since Brahmin pandits exclusively controlled the classical domain for centuries, they assumed others from non-Brahmin and lower castes had little to no chance of breaking into it.

Jashuva and Writing Upwards

By the time Gurram Jashuva started reading poetry and aspiring to become a poet, classical Telugu or granthika basha was the standard. As he came from Guntur district part of Madras presidency his education and training was seeped in the classical poetic genre. He even wrote his autobiography in the classical poetic form. Since Jashuva's father was a missionary preacher, he could access primary education in a Christian missionary school. After that, he went to a government high school where he experienced discrimination. According to him:

> All the teachers were caste Hindus: they were angry
> and used to hate us
> They never had any sympathy for us
> In classrooms, especially for us, equal to the ground,
> the old benches
> A separate space to keep our slates, books, and pieces
> of chalk
> Whenever our teachers got angry with us

---

katacharya was probably the first known Avadhani in the Telugu country. His performance at Pithapuram was a source of inspiration to others like the Devulapalli brothers.

In the late nineteenth and early twentieth centuries there was a new trend called Janta Kavulu or twin poets; Thirupati Venkata Kavulu, Koppurapu Sodarulu and Venkataramakrishna Kavulu performed Avadhanam and also participated in competitions of extempore verses and long poems. G. V. Sitapati, *The History of Telugu Literature*, pp. 116–18.

> Our untouchable status used to prevent him from
> beating us
> Indirectly we used to be saved by our status.[29]

Even in the playground, he experienced discrimination and expressed his agony; 'all caste Hindu boys used to play without barriers like brothers. By seeing them from a distance, I used to feel pained.'[30]

However, unlike his peers, he had developed an unusual interest in poetry from childhood. He mentions in his autobiography that he was inspired by the great poets of his time, Tirupati Venkata Kavulu and Koppurapu Sodarulu, two pairs of Jantakavulu. Once, Koppurapu Subba Rao visited Vindukonda. People organized a public meeting and invited people to recite poetry in his honor. Jashuva wrote poems on Subba Rao and recited them in the public meeting with the help of a Brahmin friend. Subba Rao appreciated his poems, and suddenly there was an uproar in the meeting. Many left, scolding Jashuva's Brahmin friend for bringing him to the stage. Jashuva described that humiliating experience:

> How can an untouchable enter the meeting?
> By making uproar
> Some people boycotted the meeting
> They shouted and looked like angry cobras
> I went out of the meeting with much guilt.[31]

While experiencing humiliations as a budding poet, Jashuva wanted to learn Sanskrit. Due to longstanding Brahminical prejudice, many refused to teach him, till Jupudi Hanuma Shastri showed some sympathy and taught him Sanskrit. However, those experiences did not discourage him; they made him rebel against inequality and discrimination. According to his daughter, Hemalatha Lavanam, Jashuva was denied entry into the playground by a caste Hindu boy and 'angered, Jashuva slapped him and said: Brother! This slap is not for you, but it is for your caste discrimination.'[32] Yendluri Sudhakar interpreted this incident as 'Jashuva as a child had given a tight slap

---

29 Gurram Jashua, *Naa Katha* (My Story), Jashuva Foundation, Vijayawada, 1996, p. 37.

30 Ibid., p. 46.

31 Ibid., p. 61.

32 Hemalatha Lavanam, *Maa Nannagaru* (Our Father), Vijayawada, 1995, p. 19.

against caste discrimination and as a poet, he had given *Gabbilam* which is a much more powerful ideological slap to caste Hindu society.'[33]

Jashuva faced discrimination and humiliation even after he was known as a poet. Once, he was traveling on a train. One man recognized him and requested that he recite some poems. After listening to Jashuva, he praised him and enquired about his caste. When Jashuva replied that he was a Christian, the man left, saying, 'the Saraswati got polluted.' Even in gatherings of learned poets, one was not immune to caste prejudices. Once in Kakinada, in the presence of eminent Telugu poets such as Tirupati Venkata Kavulu Tripuraneni Ramaswami Choudhary, he was humiliatingly referred to as an 'untouchable.' Jashuva replied to the humiliation with:

> The crows who are not equal to a seashell
> Out of jealousy, try to humiliate me
> But the talent I have will never leave me
> I will sing poems like a bell
> Present them to the people of Andhra like flowers.[34]

Along with arduous experiences from caste Hindu society, Jashuva faced equally painful harassment from his fellow Christians for reading Sanskrit texts and epics such as *Mahabharata* and *Ramayana*. As a result, he was dismissed from his teaching job at the school and he struggled to feed his family. Despite such bitter experiences, many other caste Hindus supported and encouraged Jashuva to pursue his poetic career by publishing his poetry, which helped him financially. Those tribulations did not defeat him; instead, they shaped his writings and made him envision a world beyond those everyday challenges. As he said, 'there were two gurus in my life; first was poverty and the second were caste and religious discrimination. The former taught me patience in life, and the latter made me revolt, but they did not enslave me. However, while facing both, I tried to prove myself as a human being. I revolted with my knife; my knife is a pen; it did not hate society but its practice.'[35] Jashuva strived to live beyond the boundaries of caste and religion:

---

33 Endluri Sudhakar, *Jashua Katha* (Jashuva's Story), Manasa Prachuranalu, Rajahmundry, 1992, p. 72.

34 Gurram Jashuva, *Kandakavyam*, Jashuva Foundation, Vijayawada, 1994, p. 64.

35 Hemalatha Lavanam, *Maa Nannagaru*, p. 10.

I will not be bound by caste and religious lines
And will not let them cage
World can judge
It will not reduce me
I am a universal human being.[36]

Gabbilam as Dalit Epic

Historically Jashuva was not the first Dalit writer in Telugu. Before him, Kusuma Dharma, Jala Rangaswamy, Nakka Chinavenkayya, Bhoi Bhemanna, and many others wrote books, novels, songs, and essays highlighting the suffering of untouchables, exposing the hypocritical behavior of caste Hindus while demanding the right to equality and exploitation free society. Their writings awakened Dalits, circulated among reformist circles and were read by sympathetic caste Hindus. However, the impact of their writings was marginal on mainstream society as they were made invisible in the course of history. Jashuva wrote nearly fifty books, and they consisted of *padya kavyas*, plays, novels, *kanda kavyas* and historical biographies. All those writings are thematically rooted in a historical context like the classical literary genre but with a conscious aim to highlight injustice and inequality. Classical literature is centered on imaginary romance or the retelling of Brahminical puranic and epic stories, intending to entertain or normalize the status quo in society. Jashuva inverted those themes and inserted social purpose into the classical genre by adding the authenticity of Dalit experience to his writings. He made it impossible for the classical elites to ignore him by choosing the poetic form. He developed a systematic critique of Hindu social and religious practices, excavated the domain of classical tradition through dark humor, and wrote about the neglected lives of people who had endured injustice and exploitation and connected them through the sufferings of untouchables. He lived in a tumultuous period in human history that witnessed world wars and radical ideologies like Marxism that influenced the Telugu literary sphere. He kept his ear to the ground to see and listen to the everyday experiences of Dalits to sharpen his pen and express their misery melodiously. Even though it is disorienting

---

36 Gurram Jashuva, *Kandakavyam,* Jashuva Sarvalabhya Sankalanamu, MaNaSu Foundation, p. 652.

to relive and recreate the suffering, he creatively expressed it by combining classical archaic language with everyday spoken words of the people, i.e., the *gramya*. Once considered offensive, these words of oppressed folks entered the lexicon of highly acclaimed classical poetry that subverted the Brahminical textual language. Because of their unique ability, Jashuva's poems were sung in village theatres and became people's songs. They even met the 'standards' of classical language, a rare feat of accomplishment.

Historically, Jashuva was avant-garde in Telugu literature. He entered their domain of classical poetry as a Dalit and proved himself a phenomenal poet. His work forced the celebrated writers of classical Telugu literature of his time, to not only recognize him but also honor him with the highest awards and shower him with felicitations. Challapalli Venkata Kavi decorated his feet with golden bracelets (*gandapenderam*) and made Jashuva sit on an elephant that took a procession in the streets. His masterpieces like *Firadosi* and *Mumtaz Mahal* explored injustice, suffering, and the anguish of losing loved ones, and will remain celebrated texts. His contemporaries like Vishwanatha Satyanarayana wrote eulogies to Brahminism and upheld caste inequality as *dharma*.[37] Added to his existing oeuvre of masterpieces was *Gabbilam*. Published in 1941 at the high noon of anti-colonial nationalism when Dalits were emerging as critical players in the nationalist movement, *Gabbilam*, as an epic text, shook the foundations of Brahminism through a critical exploration of its ideological roots and the way it perpetuates inequality and oppression. To understand its role as a seminal Dalit text, we will study four aspects of Gabbilam; a) the ideological context; b) the title of the text and its symbolic significance; c) the creation of the protagonists; and d) the thematic content of the text. They will enable us to locate the text in its historical context more precisely. Moreover, it is imperative to re-read the preface written by Jashuva to understand how far the text represents an alternative to mainstream discourse and adds to its historical significance as a Dalit epic. To quote Jashuva,

> I wrote this text by keeping Kalidasa's *Meghaduta*
> (Cloud Messenger) in mind and chose "Gabbilam"

---

37 Among many writings of Vishwanatha Satyanarayana, *Veyipadagalu*, a novel published in 1939, is considered a magnum opus in Telugu literature. It was translated into Hindi by former Prime Minister of India, P. V. Narasimha Rao for which he was feted with the Jnanpith award.

(Bat) as the title. For some readers, it might sound harsh. The protagonist in *Meghaduta* sends a message of love. My protagonist sends a searing, poignant message. The protagonist in *Meghaduta* was sentenced to one year, but my hero was sentenced from birth. For generations without any end. The hero in the *Meghaduta* was a Hindu cupid suffering from a burning desire to meet his lover. My hero is a victim of poverty that burns his stomach. That is why he says, "even to hear my tearful story; one needs a soft heart."

These lines reveal Jashuva's attempts at constructing an alternative discourse similar to the one found in classical Hindu texts like *Meghaduta*. By relating the classical discourse to the life and sufferings of an untouchable—essentially the experience of caste oppression—Jashuva subverted the dominant paradigm, which had so far excluded marginalized people's experiences from textual traditions. This social reality was articulated through the representative voice of millions of fellow untouchables. Jashuva projects himself as the ideological contender for a largely Brahminical Hindu-leaning dominant literary and intellectual tradition. In selecting the title, Jashuva draws a similarity between the life of an untouchable and that of a *gabbilam*—a bat. Just as the bat symbolizes a bad omen and is treated neither as a bird nor an animal in local culture, similarly, an untouchable is not treated as a human being despite being born human and is denied basic human needs and dignity. By drawing out the similarity between the untouchable and the bat, Jashuva powerfully depicts the reality of the life of an untouchable. In Jashuva's own words, 'Unlike the noble kings, exquisite birds like swans and parrots cannot become his messenger. That is why I chose a regular visitor to the homes of the despised, a bat, as his messenger. I hope readers will agree and understand the aptness of the title.' *Gabbilam* is thus the eponymous protagonist of the text while serving, simultaneously, as the alter ego for the poet himself and represents a collective 'untouchable' pathos.

The striking aspect of the text is the portrayal of the protagonist as a celibate hero. It is a symbolic protest against the inhuman treatment meted out to untouchables. The protagonist of *Gabbilam* says, 'When I am an outcast, why marry and give birth to another? What need there is for a wife for one so deprived.'[38] Here Jashuva reiterates the futility of conjugal life for an untouchable for whom procreation would mean perpetuating the same oppression; the lines reverberate with Jashuva's suppressed anger and frustration. In his presentation, Jashuva laments the different dimensions of caste oppression and the miserable conditions of the untouchables. Most importantly, protests against Hindu religious and social practices are often marked by scathing ridicule. While contesting the Hindu social and religious philosophy, the text is poignant while referring to the contemporary political movements such as the anti-colonial nationalism of Gandhi and Ambedkar's role in the emancipation of untouchables.

Jashuva, as a poet and intellectual, was unique, especially in the context of anti-colonial nationalism and the growing political assertion among Dalits. He maintained a cautious distance from active politics. However, his writings make it clear that he was aware of his time's political and social realities. He never joined any political organizations and did not attend nationalist Dalit or caste Hindu organized meetings. This may have been because of his precarious life riddled with financial strife and preoccupation with daily struggles to feed his family.

Moreover, his uncompromising critical bent of mind made him more inclined to expose the hypocrisy of institutions and individuals and often led him to observe things from a distance rather than get involved in murky politics. Equally important was his familial context: socially, he did not have extended family connections (the inter-caste marriage of his parents precluded this) that would have given him some economic footing to look beyond survival. That does not mean he was an apolitical person. On the contrary, he was channeling the age old history of Dalit resistance through his poetic imagination.

Politics of Translation

The practice of translation is not new to the literary history of language. However, translation is not an apolitical idealistic project. Every translation has a purpose. One needs to ask who translates and what kind of texts they translate? What is the purpose of this translation? The history of Telugu literature demonstrates that translation was a political project ushered in by

---

38 *Gabbilam*, p. 3.

Brahminical revivalism from its very beginning and was tied to translating Brahminism. Even the colonial project of language and the colonial administration's investment in the promotion of prose instead of poetry was a political project intended for the needs of governance and Christian missionaries. Even the caste Hindu reformers, especially Brahmins, used modern prose to organize politically and articulate nationalism to replace the colonial authority with their own rule. The politics of language and translation reflect the socio-economic realities and the power of the elites, and the values they promote.[39] That is why K. Purushotham says that even in the 'post-independence period Telugu literature became complaisant and self-serving.'[40]

The arrival of Dalits on the Telugu literary scene after the 1990s challenged Brahminical hegemony and questioned the absence of their voice in literature. But despite its ubiquitous presence in the Telugu public sphere, Dalit writings have been rarely translated into English. English as the language of Brahminical elites excluded Dalit writings.[41]

The translation of Telugu Dalit writings represents a necessary intervention. It questions centuries of Brahminical dominance over language and literature through an anti-caste egalitarian perspective. In this context, before I translated *Gabbilam*, it was first translated by M.B. Raja Rao in 1973 and published by the Department of Social Welfare, Andhra Pradesh. He was one of the first generation educated Dalits to enter public service through the reservation system that enabled the emergence of the Dalit middle class. However, Raja Rao's translation is literal and does not capture the nuances and meanings underlying the poetic expressions of Jashuva, as Jashuva powerfully combines classical language with colloquial words to express the everyday sufferings of Dalits in a melodious way. Unfortunately, that powerful expression is lost in Raja Rao's translation.

Moreover, Raja Rao, perhaps because of his non-academic back-

---

39 The well-known translations from Telugu into English like *Kanyasulkam*, one of the earliest plays in Telugu written by Gurajada Appa Rao and published in 1897, that dealt with the problem of bride price among Brahmins, was translated into English by C. Vijayasree and T. Vijay Kumar in 2002 and Velcheru Narayana Rao in 2007.

40 K. Purushotham, 'Evolution of Telugu Dalit Literature,' *Economic and Political Weekly*, Vol. XLV, No. 20, p. 56.

41 The first significant effort in this endeavor happened in 2016 when Oxford University Press published an anthology by K. Purushotham, Gita Ramaswami and Gogu Shyamala, *The Oxford India Anthology of Telugu Dalit Writings*, Oxford University Press, 2016.

ground, does not understand the historical and literary context of *Gabbilam*. His translation rendered the text into a verse form that makes it incomplete and at times it empties the poem of its anger and critical edge; the figure of the Dalit is someone to be pitied in this translation not someone who is assertive and resisting. Afterward, Kaki Madhava Rao, another Dalit bureaucrat, translated Gabbilam in 1996 and the Jashuva Foundation published it. Even though Madhava Rao's translation is far better than Raja Rao's, it still lacks scholarly rigor and remains a literal translation without reference to its historical and literary context. However, it does not mean that these translations have no historical value. If one reviews the long history of translation of Telugu texts, only texts written by privileged caste Hindus were translated. In this context, Dalit bureaucrats exposed to Telugu literature and well versed in the English language took to the project of translation to make the Dalit epic *Gabbilam* available to the English reading public in India to show the world power of Dalit writings.

The study and appreciation of Dalit texts have also been ignored at the international level. In the field of Telugu Studies, attention to Dalit writers has been minimal. This neglect indicates the extension of Brahminical prejudice beyond India and Dalits face marginalization even in western academia.

One of the leading Telugu translators and scholars in the west, Velcheru Narayana Rao, translated selected poems from *Gabbilam* to include in the verses of twentieth-century Telugu poetry in translation. A careful reading of Narayana Rao's translation clarifies that he is selective about the verses. His translation has transformed powerful verses into lifeless cultural descriptions. His translation suggests for us that the translator has the power to subvert the original political meaning of the words and cleanse the text of its radical anti-Brahminical expression. I will analyze a poem from his translation to illustrate the politics of subversion. For example, Narayana Rao translated the third verse from Gabbilam as:

> He makes shoes
> to protect the feet of his masters
> who keep him poor
> and keep him low[42]

---

42 Velcheru Narayana Rao, *Hibiscus On The Lake: 20th Century Telugu Poetry from India*, University of Wisconsin Press, 2003, p. 214.

The Telugu original of the poem reads as:

Muppu ghatinci vini galimin gabalinchi Dhehamul
Bippi yonarchu Nee Bharata Viruni paadamu
Kandukudagaa
Jeppulu Gutti Jeevanamu Seyunu Gaani Nira-
karimpa Le
Depudu Nappu Vaddadi Sumee Bharata Vani
Veeni Sevaku

The above poem is rich in content and exposes the exploitation endured by Dalits. The actual translation is:

Caste Hindus imposed many hardships upon him
Tried to destroy his caste
Tortured and squeezed his body
But he never rebelled against them
Instead, he stitched shoes to protect the feet of great
upper caste heroes of the nation
And led life as a dutiful man
This country, Bharat, is in his debt

Narayana Rao's translation toned down the anger and the radical message hidden in the poem. When one recites the poem in Telugu, it moves the heart of an ordinary listener. For example, Jashuva uses the expression *pippi onarchu* that means 'squeeze dry to pith' (like a sugar cane) that expresses the ontological violence inflicted on a Dalit body through exploitation and violence. Jashuva by bringing the lived experience of a Dalit humanizes the poetry. But Narayana Rao's translation removes the exploitation and makes it abstract and conveys neither its temper nor expresses the essence. Narayana Rao's translation emptied the verses of their radical spirit to fit them into the mainstream rhythm of poetry that merely describes the status of Dalits and treats them as objects of pity, not agents of revolution or resistance. Thus, the academic translations such as Narayana Rao's fit into larger Brahminical politics of downplaying the radicalism and the historical meaning of Dalit poetry. A translation is like retelling a story. It involves the translator's faithfulness to the original story and maintains the integrity of the original author's ethical intention. A translator, like an interpreter, can turn and twist the original meaning and purpose of the text. One can easily focus on the beautiful play with the language and arrangement of poetic narration without any attention to the social message in the text. Thus, in the mainstream Brahminical reading, *Gabbilam*'s achievement has been primarily in terms of its poetic value, not as a social text that contended the dominant ideology. In contrast, Raja Rao and Madhava Rao were not great translators. Still, they were passionate about the content of *Gabbilam* and its revolutionary role in bringing a Dalit protagonist into mainstream Telugu literature.

References

Gurram Jashuva's Writings

Jashuva, Gurram, *Himadhamarkadhara Parinayam,* 1917

________, *Chidananda Prabhatam,*(play), 1921

________, *Kushalopakyanam,* (play) Guntur, 1923

________, *Rukmini Kalyanam*, Sri Kanyaka Parmeshwar Mudrakshara Shala, Guntur, 1923.

________, *Sri Kanyaka Parameshwari*, 1924.

________, *Druva Vijayam,* Chandrika Mudrakshara Shala, Guntur, 1925.

________, *Shivaji,* Guntur, 1926.

________, *Sri Sharada Smruthi,* 1928.

________, *Phiradowsi,* Andhra University Press, Vishakhapatnam, 1932.

________, *Swapna Katha,* Book Lovers Private Limited, Guntur, 1934.

________, *Anadha* (Orphan), Book Lovers Private Limited, Guntur, 1935.

________, *Khandakavyam* (first part), Book Lovers Private Limited, Guntur, 1937.

________, *Khandakavyam* (second part), Book Lovers Private Limited, Guntur, 1937.

________, *Khandakavyam* (third part), Venkatrama and Co., Bejavada, 1946

________, *Khandakavyam* (fourth part), Kondapally Veeravenkaiah and Sons, Rajahmundry, 1950.

________, *Khandakavyam* (fifth part), Hemalatha Lavanam Publishers, Vijayawada, 1952.

________, *Gabbilam – 1,* Thota Gopala Krishnaiah Publications, Guntur, 1941.

________, *Gabbilam – 2,* Thota Gopala Krishnaiah Publications, Guntur, 1946.

________, *Mumtaj Mahal,* Hemalatha Lavanam Publishers, Vijayawada, 1943.

________, *Khandeeshikudu,* Hemalatha Lavanam Publishers, Vijayawada, 1945.

________, *Terachatu* (drama), Venkatrama and Co., Bejavada, 1946.

________, *Veerabhai* (historical drama), Sri Sathyanarayana Book Depot, Rajahmundry, 1947.

________, *Netaji* (biography of Subash Chandra Bose), Kondapally Veeravenkaiah and Sons, Rajahmundry, 1947.

________, *Bapuji* (biography of M.K.Gandhi), Kondapally Veeravenkaiah and Sons, Rajahmundry, 1948.

________, *Chinnanaayakudu,* Prabhu and Co., Guntur, 1948.

________, *Swayamvaram,* Hemalatha Lavanam Publishers, Vijayawada, 1950.

________, *Veerabai,* Sri Kondapally Mudrashala, Rajahmundry, 1950.

________, *Rastrapooja,* Hemalatha Lavanam Publishers, Vijayawada, 1953.

________, *Kothalokam,* Hemalatha Lavanam Publishers, Vijayawada, 1957.

________, *Naa Katha – 1* (autobiography) Book Lover's Private Limited, Guntur, 1952.

________, *Naa Katha – 2* (autobiography) Book Lover's Private Limited, Guntur, 1962

________, *Naa Katha – 3* (autobiography) Book Lover's Private Limited, Guntur, 1966

________, *Kristhucharitra,* I. S. P. C. K Press, Madras, 1963.

________, *Musaafarlu,* Hemalatha Lavanam Publishers, Vijayawada, 1963.

________, *Nagarjunasagar,* Hemalatha Lavanam Publishers, Vijayawada, 1966.

________, *Firadosi,* Andhra University Press, Valtheru, 1971.

________, *Naa Katha,* Nava Mudranalu Publications, Vijayawada, 1976.

Writings on Gurram Jashuva

Amulya Sree, *Jashuva Gabbilam Rayabaram*, Ratna Jyothi Publications, Guntur, 1995.

Bhaskarachowdari, B., *Jashuva Jeevitha Kavitha Prasthanam*, Samatha Publications, Chittoor, 1979

Bhaskarachowdari, B., *Jashuva Kruthulu Samalochana,* Samatha Publications, Chittoor, 1982.

Bhaskarachowdari, B., *Bharathiya Sahitya Nirmathalu Jashuva,* Sahitya Academy, New Delhi, 1996.

Gopi, N., *Jashuva Shata Jayanthi,* Jashuva Foundation, Hyderabad. 1995.

Govardhan, Borra, *Kavi Kokila Gurram Jashuva Nakatha*, Arts and Letters Publications, 2018.

Lavanam, Hemalata, *Maa Nannagaru,* Saisudha Printers, Vijayawada, 2003.

Lavanam, Hemalata and Endluri Sudhakar, *Maa Nannagaru* (essays), Telugu Academy, Hyderabad, 2011.

Jangaiah, Boya, *Vishwanarudu Gurram Jashuva,* Vishalandra Publications, Hyderabad.

Jayaramulu, B., *Gabbilam Oka Parishilana*, Kavadiguda, Hyderabad, 1992.

Madhujyothi, Kolakaluri, *Gurram Jashuva*, C. P. Brown Academy, Hyderabad, 2010.

Mallaiah, Kaluva, *Gabbilam* (*Gurram Jashuva Tatvika Swapanam*), Telugu Academy, Hyderabad. 2012.

Mallaiah, Kaluva, *Gurram Jashuva Kruthulu ,Sampradayam, Navyata*, Jashuva Research Center, Telugu Academy, Hyderabad. 2013

Mohan Rao, Addepally, Mahakavi Jashuva Pragathisheelatha, Kalatmakatha, Jashuva 120th Birth Anniversary Committee, Guntur, 2015.

Nirmalananda, Jashuva Kavithva Tatvam (collected essays), Jana Sahithi Publications, 1997.

Padmarao, Katti, *Jashuva Saamajika Tatvam 'Gabbilam – Firadousi Vishle-shana*, Lokayutha Publications, Guntur, 1996.

Padmarao, Katti, *Dalitha Sahitya Vaadam Jashuva*, Lokayutha Publications, Guntur, 1994.

Prabhakara Rao, M.S., *Jashuva Sahityam Manavataavadam*, Jashuva Research Center, Telugu Academy, Hyderabad, 2013

Prabhakara Rao, M.S., Madhura Srinathudu Jashuva, Mahakavi Jashuva Jayanthi Samithi, Narsapuram, 1981.

Rayudu, M.V., *Jashuva (SarvaLabyaSankalanam)*, MaNaSu Foundation, Benguluru, 2013.

Satyanarayana Reddy. A, *Jashuva Sahitya Samalochanam*, Jashuva Research Center, Telugu Academy, 2014.

Satyavathi, Tella., *Hetuvaadi Jashuva* (collected essays), Harika Publications, Guntur, 2001.

Simmanna, Velamana., *Jashuva Firadousi Oka Parishodana*, Dalit Literary Center, Vishakhapatnam, 1999.

Sudhakar, Endluri. *Jashuva Katha*, Manasa Publications, Rajahmundry, 1992.

Sudhakar, Endluri, *Kathanayakudu Jashuva* (biography), Telugu Academy, Hyderabad, 2012.

Sundara Rao, R. R. *Mahakavi Vyaktitvam – Kavitvam*, Sowvaartika Publications, Hyderabad, 1986.

Thiyador, B., *Navayuga Kavichakravarthi*, Mahakavi Jashuva Jayanthi Samithi, Narsapuram, 1979.

Varaprasad, T., *Jashuva Sahityam Samajika Nyayam*, Jashuva Research Center,

Telugu Academy, 2014.

Yadagiri, K., *Jatiyakavi Jashuva,* Jashuva Research Center, Telugu Academy, 2014.

Yadagiri, K., *Jashuva Sahitya Tatva Vivechana* (collected essays), Jashuva Research Center, Telugu Academy, Hyderabad, 2012.

Yadagiri, K., *Jashuvatho Anubhavaalu Jganapakaalu,* Jashuva Research Center, Telugu Academy, Hyderabad, 2014.

PREFACE TO PART I

Dear Compatriots!

I wrote this text by keeping Kalidasa's *Meghaduta* in mind. The title 'Gabbilam' (Bat) might sound harsh to readers. The protagonist in *Meghaduta* sends a message of love. My protagonist sends a searing, poignant message. The protagonist in *Meghaduta* was sentenced to one year, but my hero was sentenced from birth. For generations without any end. The hero in *Meghaduta* was suffering from a burning desire to meet his lover. My hero is a victim of poverty that burns his stomach. That is why he says, 'even to hear my tearful story; one needs a soft heart.' Unlike the noble kings, exquisite birds like swans and parrots cannot become his messenger. That is why I chose a regular visitor to the homes of the despised, a bat, as his messenger. I hope readers will agree and understand the aptness of the title. The bat entered his home and extinguished the lamp. He prayed to her to convey his tearful story to God Eshwara.

Nevertheless, he intended the bat to tour around the country to tell his tearful story and worship the nation. Thus, the route I chose to Kailasa deviates from the ordinary course and should not be considered a defect. On the contrary, if the world can appreciate this creation, I'll feel rewarded for the hard work. I feel lucky that aesthete Sri Kalluri Chandramouli Choudary, Guntur district board president, and nationalist, visited my village and listened to the text. As a result, he agreed to bear the publication cost that enabled the completion of the text. I feel very grateful for his generosity.

— Jashuva, 1941.

PART I

An Untouchable Odyssey

There are four cardinal directions in the universe
This untouchable has none to claim
He is the last son of Mother India
Innocent enough to be content with penury
Forgets all his suffering
With a fistful of rice
To fill his burning stomach

He lives in the southern corner of Tanjore [43]
To where Telugu poetry migrated at a tender age
A kingdom ruled by Raghunatha Rayulu
Under his patronage, Telugu language and literature flourished
Despite poverty, he led a life of honesty and moral integrity

Caste Hindus imposed many hardships upon him
Tried to destroy his caste
Tortured and squeezed his body
But he never rebelled against them
Instead, he stitched shoes to protect the feet of great
          upper caste heroes of the nation
And led life as a dutiful man
This country, Bharat[44] is in his debt

Without his labor
Even the crops hesitate to grow
By sweating day and night, he feeds the world
But has nothing to eat

To cleanse the muck of untouchability that soils his head
Even the holiest Ganga has no compassion
His touch is considered polluting
If he handles the offerings
The trinity of Gods must starve

---

43 Now known as Thanjavur.

44 Article 1 of the Indian constitution defines 'India that is Bharat, shall be a union of
states.' The reference to Bharat as an ancient identity indicates a geographical notion rather
than a religious identity, such as Hindu, and reflects the deep historical and socially con-
scious engagement of Gurram Jashuva.

In this holy land of *karma*
They feed milk to snakes and sugar to ants
Even the goddess of justice will shake in his presence

There is no god to uplift him
How can one expect mortal humans to show compassion?
He does not know
What sin he has committed

The demon of poverty sucks his blood
The four hooded Hindu cobra[45]
Hisses with anger in fear of wind from his side[46]

---

45 The four hooded cobra is a metaphor for the four *varnas* of caste. All four *varnas*, from which all other *jatis* (castes) originate, practise untouchability, discrimination, violence and hatred towards Dalits.

46 In spatial organization of villages, 'untouchables' are always made to live downstream. The savarnas (caste Hindus) also ensure that wind from Dalit houses should not blow towards the direction of touchable castes' houses by making them live outside the village. If Dalits live closer to the caste Hindu neighborhoods, their house's main entrance is not allowed to face the main roads of the village. They also secure caste Hindu neighborhoods with walls or rubbish dumps that mark our Dalits neighborhoods.

Born a slave and an outcaste
How can he think of a wife and children?
Not wanting to bring them into the world of despair
He lived his life as a celibate

He toiled in the field the entire day
From dawn onwards
Returning home at dusk after sending the Sun to sleep
After eating porridge
He laid down to rest on a broken cot

Like an elephant in a rut
The darkness of the night
Covered the earth and heaven
In that holy hour
God Eshwara finished his dance
And recited auspicious prayers

At that hour, without a nose or face
A bat flew into his hut
Like a black round ball
Wind from her wings
Extinguished the castor oil lamp

In that darkness
He saw the bird
Fly like a demonic disk
And his mind wandered into new imaginations

In this mad caste obsessed world
Other than birds and insects
He has no near and dear
Sensing her friendliness
He decided to share the uninspiring stories of his life
Do the poor have any friends besides these lowly beasts and insects?
Will they have any Cakravaka geese to elaborate on their warm tears?

Oh, queen of bats, welcome to my house
You live in the most auspicious temples
You perform prayers standing upside-down
You are visiting an untouchable who has no
          respect in society
It is not a good omen for your children

In the terrible dark of night
When the earth has closed her eyes and fallen
          into deep sleep
And forgotten her body
What are you searching for in my house?
You will not find any ray of hope or happiness here

This is a forbidden house of an untouchable
If you enter, the world will cast you out, my sister!
You eat food offered to gods and goddesses!
But have entered the house of a poor man
          who has nothing to eat
The Sun moves between East and West
The cycle of life continues
However, the milk of the sacred cow of Santana Dharma[47]
Never reaches this poor man
Even the gods heed the dictums of the rich and powerful
And keep silent about the sufferings of the poor
Indeed! This is a heartless world

They spend thousands of rupees to celebrate
          the marriage of dolls
Yet they refuse to put a grain of rice in the bowl of a beggar
In a country where there are millions of gods to rob
Who will feed the hungry stomach of a wretched person?

---

47 The ideology of Sanatan Dharma, the foundational basis of Hindu Brahminical philosophy, justifies the denial of basic material needs such as food, decent living spaces, knowledge/education, and human dignity to Dalits.

Religious teachers claim to possess supreme knowledge
They are wily
And condemn truthful people as sinners and criminals
They claim to show the way to heaven
But without my existence, the chariot of Vedic philosophy
        cannot move forward

You meditate in the day upside down like a hermit
Live a life of contentment with your family
You feel anguish at the plight of paupers like us
And venture out in the night to console us
Oh, saintly bird! You deserve all the respect in the world

Seeing my plight
Hearts of mountains split
And their tears ran like streams to console me
But there is no sign of a teardrop in the eyes of my countrymen

You are related to divine sages like Valakhilyas
They are luminaries of yogic teaching
By birth, you mediate and have a tender heart
As a well-wisher of others
You have separated from the King of birds the eagle
I salute and relate my story

In the lull of the night
The night has put the world to sleep
But she forgot about the untouchable
Inflicted with the incurable disease of untouchability

Selfish people relish the fruits of my labor
And use *karma* theory to seal my mouth
What is *karma*?
Find out from the God Shiva
Reasons for *karma*'s hatred of me

Oh, Ascetic Queen of birds!
When you hang upside down inside the temple
You will be closer to the ear of the God Shiva
Make sure the priest is not around
When you recount the story of my life

The thick braid of lady night whitens
Your owl neighbors cease their hunt and return to their homes.
Even at this time, if the priests listen to you
They will chastise you
Even the God Shiva might be angered by you

The touch of tender breeze from your wings
Comforts my drained body with kindness
I can never reward your affection
I am indebted to you forever

Oh, bird! To express pride in response to your salutations
I am unworthy
Even to appreciate your art
I do not possess a caste status
I am not a rich person with an overfilled stomach
To consider you, out of selfishness, as a tool
I am not a religious preacher

To scorn and dominate you[48]
The world despises you
Because you have the nature of an animal and a bird
Destitute, I do not care for those old fashioned ideas
            of ill omens
Queen of bats! You came and consoled my heart!
Narrate my suffering to the bearer of the trident, the God Shiva

Justice has no fear
Truth has no death
If God is the creator
You are his creation
Thus, you never have to fear to speak the truth in front of Him

Give my greetings to the Creator
No human can enter His abode
Even if He lives in the Himalayas
You visit Him there
Only a day's journey for a big-hearted one like you

---

48 While translating, I often read poetry and listened to African American singers to connect the echoes of Dalit experience. I found a fascinating connection between Jashuva and Louis Daniel Armstrong, a trumpeter and vocalist; his song 'Black and Blue' resonates with Jashuva's poems, and I took the word 'scorn' from it: 'Louis Armstrong - Black and Blue,' YouTube, January 25, 2013, https://youtu.be/2LDPUfbXRLM.

On your way to visit Shiva in Kashi
While passing through clouds
Take a route through the Milky Way
You might even encounter Shiva on the journey
Be careful! Do not lose your way
Arrive before the sunrise
So that the light will not blind you

When you fly in the sky
Using black umbrella-shaped wings
The rain god will sprinkle drops of water like pearls

Put your feet on earth
When the sunset's rays glow, the soil turns red and bright
Feel honored by the touch of fresh air from the running streams
Travel on the clouds that collide with mountains and split
Float on the waves in the heavenly Ganga
Where royal swans and their cygnets swim

Eat the sweetest fruits tasted by parrots
Forget all worries about crooked world for some time

When you hear my tearful story
Your heart will melt
You vowed to eat herbivorous food
And have a heart filled with the radiance of kindness

You have unique qualities
Bear children and feed them milk
You came to rescue me like an angel
Will you listen to my submission?

Oh, blessed bird! Your children will appreciate your
                unhesitating generosity
With the consent of your husband
Swing in the mountains and jungles where the God Shiva lives
And return successfully

Oh, beauty! Light snacks and little water are enough to fill your slight
          belly
You can roam anywhere in the world without difficulty
Unlike me, you are not a slave by birth
Not worrying about time
On the way, visit temples and holy places
Forests and mountains cannot hamper your journey
If you encounter cyclones, take shelter in **dharmasatram**[49]
An unfortunate such as me is not allowed to enter those places
Even to escape from lightning

---

49 Historically *dharmasatrams* (rest houses) were built on trade routes that also connect holy places to which ascetics, traders and common people undertook long pilgrimages and rested during nights and inclement weather. They were established and maintained by the state. Emperor Ashoka mentions in his Seven Rock Pillar Edicts, the establishment of *dharmasatrams* as an ethical responsibility of the state. Ven. S. Dhammika, 'The Edicts of King Ashoka,' King Ashoka: His Edicts and His Times, accessed December 23, 2021, https://www.cs.colostate.edu/~malaiya/ashoka.html.

You can eat delicious fruits in the forests
Sleep in the rest houses
On the way, you will come across many holy lands

Beautiful Tanjore is on the way
In the court of Raghunatha Rayulu
Telugu literature blossomed

After the departure of Krishna Devaraya
This loss brought darkness in all directions
The goddess of literature used her pen as a stick to direct
And walked towards Tanjore
At this juncture, Chemakuri Venkata Kavi[50]
He made *slesha*[51] fashionable in Telugu poetry
Romantic poetry blossomed
Poets such as Kshetrayya, through their devotional rigor
Took Telugu literary tastes to otherworldly realms
The court of Raghunatha Rayalu was famed for the presence
        of legendary Telugu poets

You will be thrilled to see the Saraswathi Mahal library
There are no rivals to it Head north for the man who intends to pass out
        of the Dravida lands
The unceasing heroism that scours the Telugu borderlands
Will be a feast for the eyes
Texts composed at that court set standards for the Telugu language
The *Mahabharata* composed there was considered the fifth *Veda*
The poet Tikkana used *Mahabharata*
Bathe in the greatly esteemed Penna river
Offer your salutations to Nellore
Where Tikkana Somayaji dwelled

50 Chemakura Venkata Kavi was a court poet of Raghunatha Raya, founder of the Thondaman Dynasty. Raghunatha Raya patronized Telugu, Tamil, Marathi and Kannada poets. Nicholas Dirks in his *The Hollow Crown: The Ethnohistory of an Indian Kingdom* (Cambridge University Press, 1987) retraces the history of the kingdom from the sixteenth century onwards. Chemakuri Venkata Kavi used humor and intrigue in every poem he wrote.
51 *Slesha* means double entendres.

And achieved everlasting renown
For teaching the fifteen *parvas* of the Bharata
Ensnared in the wild jungles of Sanskrit that lacks *yati* or *prasa*
How to be Telugu?
It seems the exquisite[52] women of Nellore
Distract even the great poets by their mischievous deeds
Find out the truth of that rumor

You must visit the fabled Hampi, the capital of the Vijayanagar empire
Once, it was a paradise for Telugu kings
Now it is a lost glory
But you will find your relatives living in nests in those ruins
Still a delightful place to visit

Women were not veiled in that city
They used to sell heaps of precious stones in the wholesale market
Oh, bird! Conquering hero Krishnadevaraya ruled from
      Telugu land with splendor

---

52 'Nellore Nerajana', the phrase used in the original, is an expression that has no equivalent in English.

Goosebumps will appear when we recall those glorious times

When enemies, out of jealousy, chopped bodies into pieces
The fierce look in the eyes of the lion-headed god Narasimha
      remained unchanged
If you stand near him even for a minute
You will be praised as fearless

On the summit of the mountain, see the statue of Lord Ganesh
It reminds you of an actual elephant
His paunch is so smooth that even a beetle cannot hold its grip
Vijayanagar—that city of knowledge—is the repository of sculptures
      like Ganesh
Our Telugu wastrels surrendered that cultural wealth to the people
      of Tungabhadra
Shed one teardrop as a tribute to the loss of that cultural heritage

Gracious Krishna Devaraya rode on Persian horses
Harnessed in arcs, these horses were used to plow
The seeds of victory by the Andhra brothers
And filled the grandeur of those victories in granary baskets

Now those brave royals of Rayala
Do not join the processions in Vidyanagar
Parsi horse traders are not pitching tents
To sell valuable horses
Excited giant elephants will not perform gymnastic tricks
      with large iron rods
No more do troops of Telugu soldiers or European cannons fill this place
Oh, ascetic bird! Andhra's kingdom that once used to glitter
      with diamonds
Perished in the sixteenth century
Darkness descended on the kingdom of Krishna Devaraya
There is no dawn, even to this day

On the way, visit the Guntur region; your life will be enriched
It was vanquished many times by ruthless rulers
You will come across the magnificent city of Kancharla, built
        by Srikrishna Gandharva
He reduced to dust the fort of Vinukonda King Raya Bhaskar
With a kick, he shook it to the ground
He ended the unrivaled rule of the Palnati kings
He threw the famed Kondaviti kingdom into a well
With his shining steel sword
And washed his hands in their warm blood

During the Bhaskaras[53]
Guntur enjoyed prosperity
Like the Sun, it brought brightness to the land
The region experienced a period of prominence
Famed cock-fight competitions are symbols of bravery
Telugus pour their blood into this wasteful sport
In the yearly festivities at Karempudi
Cocks, feet affixed with rusted knives fight and entertain
        people even today

Kondaviti kings encouraged great compositions in Telugu
And supported poets generously
Those great deeds grieve
On top of the mountains

---

53 Here Jashuva refers to Rayani Bhaskarudu and Hulakka Bhaskarudu. Rayani Bhaskara was a famous minister also known as Kataya Vema Reddy in the fourteenth century. He appears in many sources and is known as a scholar, poet and administrator. For details see *Rayanabhaskaramantri Charitram: A History of Rayani Bhaskarudu, A Scholar, Poet and Financial Administrator at the Beginning of 15th Century*, Saraswata Series, pp. 55. Cocanada, 1900 and Velcheru Narayana Rao and Sanjay Subrahmanyam, 'Notes on Political Thought in Medieval and Early Modern South India', *Modern Asian Studies*, Vol. 43, No. 1, 2009, pp. 175–210. Hulakka Bhaskara produced the Telugu *Ramayana*. For details see Velcheru Narayana Rao and David Shulman, *Classical Telugu Poetry*, University of California Press, Berkley, 2002.

Vemana was the greatest poet of the Reddy kingdom
Disillusioned with everyday life
He wandered in the streets like a vagabond
His elegant, spontaneous poetry was delightful to hear
Each word had a wealth of meaning
And thoughtful provocation

With clouds as witnesses, continue your journey along
      the Krishna Valley
Visit all the spiritual sanctuaries
And you must see Rajamahendravaram, the birthplace
      of Nannayya
He was considered the grandfather of all Telugu poets
Literary talents brightened that place
Under the rule of Chalukyan kings, it was also known
      as the chest of precious stones

Nannayya heard the echoes of Kannada literature
And witnessed its colorful presence everywhere
It pained his heart
And prompted him to produce the first Telugu treatises
Rajamahendravaram was the birthplace and its witness

An erudite scholar
Nannayya retold the story of the Pandavas
He rendered the *Mahabharata* into two and a half halves
In a melodious and tasteful Telugu form

The famed King Vishnuvardhana's times
The river Gautami Ganga[54] will welcome you
The grass of that wetland gave birth to chivalrous people
      and is an attractive place

---

54 Another name for river Godavari is Gautami Ganga.

You might not have heard the sorrowful tale of *Sarangadhara*[55]
A victim of wicked politics

He had to carry a wrongful mark on his head
As a reminder of the injustice done to this young prince
Pigeons groan around the neck of Queen Chitrangi
            in a mournful voice

---

55 *Sarangadhara* is an epic historical fictional story based on the life of King Rajaraja Na-
rendra, ruler of the eastern Vengi Chalukya kingdom. In the seventeenth century, Chemak-
ura Venkata Kavi wrote *Sarangadhara Chaitram* and it inspired many modern Telugu
poets to rewrite the story in many versions. Gurajada Appa Rao wrote the story in English
and published it in 1883 in *Indian Leisure Hour*. Chemakura Venkata Kavi, *Sarangadha-
ra Charitramu*, Sri Rama Press, Madras, 1910.

Spurn the pretext of distance
Don't be lazy and and fail to visit holy Draksharamam
The Lord Shiva known as Bhimeshwara is an incomparably
        merciful God
He dances relentlessly with bells tied to his feet
He might emancipate my community
You must witness his omnipotence

Oh, Bat! Look at you!
Queens there praise you as a beautiful round musk
And think you were a gift sent by the poet Srinath
They will fall in love with your charm

Lotuses like diamonds adorned the chariot of waves
The Godavari River runs to meet the eternal God,
        the Indian Ocean
Go along with the Godavari and see all the cities
        in southern India

Draksharamam replicates the holy Kashi
It is a center of miracles
It is an abode of Lord Siva
He keeps poison and nectar in his throat together

The French lord Bussy crushed the valor of the Velama kings[56]
Flames from their fearless fights are visible
And the groans of their tenacity can be heard
The fortress at Bobbili will thrill your body
And the warm blood in your veins will run with courage

---

56 Charles Joseph Patissier de Bussy, the Governor General of French East India Company, supported the ruler of Vizianagaram in defeating the ruler of Bobbili in 1757. For more details on the Battle of Bobbili and the role of the French East India Company, see Michael Katten's *Colonial Lists/Indian Power: Identity Politics in Nineteenth Century Telugu-Speaking India*, Columbia University Press, 2005.

Without any pity
They tie knives to my feet and do royal sport
Without hearing my plaint
That unending darkness will not go
As though it will not dawn
At that moment rooster is already flapping its wings and crowing
KOKKARO KO and announces the crack of dawn

At Vizianagaram, the capital of Pusapati kings
See the caravan of horses
When they march like an arranged garland
The earth will shake and make marvelous sounds

Those paramount royals
Drew the borders of their kingdom with swords, up to Orissa[57]
And erected victory pillars at Potnuru
Angels stood on the column and sang in praise of those Andhra kings

As you go through Bobbili
Once you cross jungles
You will notice the fading glories of the Telugu people
And Oriya atmosphere appears

Once you reach Lake Chilka
It will captivate you
Like pure Telugu, the sweet water of the lake spreads in all directions
It will delight and quench your thirst

Swaying breezes from the lake
Bring beautiful waves to the shore
When they pull back
It reminds us of the poets' playful celebration of nature's romance

---

57 Now called Odisha.

On your way, there are the cities of Nalanda and Pataliputra
They were Buddhist ruins
You will behold golden palaces in which Magadha queens lived
It was also the holy land of Shakyamuni, the Buddha
Where his preaching of non-violence flowed like a stream of nectar

Varanasi is a foremost place of redemption among the holy places
You will have salvation if you eat at the temple of Annapurna Devi
The goddess of food and nourishment

As a cousin to all rivers and the eldest wife of the Indian Ocean
River Ganga comes with streams of water
Goddess Annapurna[58] along with her husband Shiva will worship
And welcome you as their guest
Great poets and intellectuals who swam the ocean
        of knowledge resided there
Sage Vyasa, the author of *Vedas* and *Puranas*, lived
        there with his pupils
Even Lord Shiva lived there once

---

58 Parvati, wife of God Eshwara, is known by many names including Annapurna.

In the city of Delhi
The Mughal green crescent flag flew high in the sky
And castles kissed the clouds

Delhi used to be known as Hastinapura
In the era of Dvapara Yuga
King Dharma Raja of Mahabharata ruled
He conducted incomparable sacrificial rituals
One must visit the city to sense its glory
Its scents of luxurious perfumes

At this place, legendary Bhima tied the hair of Draupadi
Soaked in the blood of his enemies
It is here Nader Shah massacred many
He made an entire country weep in pain
It is here Shah Jahan installed his Green Peacock Throne
It is here Prithviraj was awarded
King Jayachandra's daughter's hand in marriage for displaying valor
Delhi keeps centuries of royal tales in its belly
It floated in the blood of royal dynasties
Still keeps a beautiful smile, and its hair has not greyed yet

Sultans and their wives lived in palaces decorated with precious stones
They ate sumptuous dishes on diamond-studded plates
              with pearl designs
They lived in luxury and spent time swinging
While people starved

Qutb Minar built by Qutb-ud-din Aibak
A great tower and was once the tallest
It stood the test of time
And its artistic sculpture remains intact
Kalindi, the goddess of Yamuna and wife of Lord Krishna
With her swarthy complexion and delicate waves
With precious breeze will welcome you
You will hear a unique story in Delhi

Of Babur, the founder of the Mughal empire
When his son Humayun fell ill
Persuaded almighty Allah through prayer to cure his son
Even now, people in the city tell this captivating story

Oh, bird! The Taj Mahal is the most beautiful structure
It was the mournful teardrop of Shah Jahan
To lay to rest his beloved wife Mumtaz Begum

Oh, lovely bird! Go through Kurukshetra
Magical Lord Krishna preached the *Bhagavad Gita* there
That explained the essence of *Vedas*
Bodhisattva is worthy of being praised by eminent kings
His heart longed to establish peace in the world
In the middle of the night, he left palatial luxuries
He spent the rest of his life with a begging bowl
You must stay for two days at the holy city of Kapilavastu
Your life will be enriched

You fly in the Lumbini garden
With the fragrance of flowers and rhythmic sounds
            of water
 In which the golden swans revered by Gautama swam
By dropping off flowers, Gokshira will welcome you

You can have glimpses of Gautama Buddha in many
            ancient Indian sculptures
One can perfect the principles of peace by following
            in his footsteps
You will learn about the literary contributions of the
            Buddhist poet Amarsimha
You will see the ruins of the city of Kapilavastu

You will encounter the erased history of the Mauryas
Even nature will narrate their greatness
Shed some warm tears in their memory

From there, if you try to go up north
The Himalayan mountains will block your way
Many white lords tried to scale those mountains and died
We do not know the magic of that snow
Still, those dead bodies remained intact

As mountains melt and fall into the valleys
They kill many creatures
Oh! Glorious bird!
It is true, friendship with the powerful will
always harm the powerless

Sitting on top of Mount Everest
One can draw the map of India
Stars illuminate its beauty
Beauty that cannot be captured even by
the most imaginative artists

The sky route on which the flamingos fly
It is on top of the mountains
Touching the North and South stars
And you cannot reach there
Gods move in groups on those silver mountains
They are visible from one side

On your pilgrimage to the holy place Kailasa[59]
Lord Shiva, the god of snow, will bless you
He might send a message to his daughter
        and son-in-law with you
Convey his message; words are not a burden to carry

Parvati's youngest son Kumaraswamy
As a child, while learning archery
Made fantastic holes in the mountain
They formed a cave to the north side of the Taraka Hill

As a sign of friendship with the snow mountains
Put a dot of snow on your forehead
That will be an endorsement for Shiva
Indeed, contacts with great people will never go to waste

Through snow mountains, once you cross the clouds
You will see the heavenly abode of Lord Shiva
You will not find *apsaras*[60] dancing there
Now that land is in the hands of strange kings called Lamas[61]

---

59 Kailasa is the abode of God Shiva.

60 *Gandharvas* and *apsaras* are often associated as either lovers or married couples and have been conceived of as a class of semidivine beings throughout the history of Hinduism. According to the *Aitareyabrāhmannna* (3.31), they form a group besides 'gods and men, serpents and fathers.' See, Thomas Oberlies, 'Gandharvas and Apsarases,' Brill (Brill, May 29, 2018), https://referenceworks.brillonline.com/entries/brill-s-encyclopedia-of-hinduism/gandharva-s-and-apsaras-es-COM_1030330.

61 Tibetan Buddhist monks.

The Dalai Lamas remain celibate all their lives
They renounce worldly pleasure and seek spiritual liberation
They wear long caps on their heads
No one ventures into that area without their permission
There is no restriction for a bird like you to enter any place

Although bad superstitions are there
Still the Buddhist forests do not let the cruel tiger
            of untouchability roam

Water in the lake of Manasa Sarovar is incomparable
            in taste and purity
River Ganga, like a child, takes its course from it
And runs up and down in the mountains
Here one can appreciate its beauty fully

Large yaks and rhinoceroses roam in that mountainous region
They enjoy the streams
And they use sharp arrow-like horns to stab
Even the carcasses of tigers are found with the holes made
            with their horns

No lake can match the ocean-like Manasa Sarovar
Powerful waves come and go
Forceful waves hit the mountains and kill big fish and crabs
Their carcasses form heaps making it difficult to walk

In those days, a celestial swan acted as a messenger
            to Nala and Damayanti
Her relatives live in that lake
And narrate the love stories of Nala Damayanti

In the moonlight, grazing on green pasture
You will spot Nandi the bull walking in the silver mountains
You will reach the forest of Shiva the Gajasura
The killer of the elephant demon
Flowers shaped like the moon will be visible
Anyway, you know these things
I need not educate you

In the forest, pay homage to the bow and arrow wielding Chenchus[62]
Lord Shiva comes to reward his devotees
And transforms himself and mixes with that savage tribe
He blinds the human eye and makes mischief to confound them

Every day many people meditate there
They are gracious and appreciate the talents of others
Nowadays, that quality is rare

---

62 Chenchus are an indigenous community based in Telugu speaking regions of Andhra Pradesh, Telangana, Karnataka and Odisha. They live as hunter gatherers and were branded as a criminal tribe by the British colonial state because their wandering lifestyles were seen as a threat to the stability of the state. Interestingly Jashuva locates them in the Himalayas and uses prejudiced language of contempt by referring to them as savages.

Nearby, you will see smoke from heaps of ash
Those are three cities burnt by Lord Shiva
To end the evil desires of demons
Indeed, strange is the power of sin

After worshiping Shiva
The blue clouds move to bring the first drops of rain
Hear the roar of chariot carrying elephants
That scared the wives of the buffalo demon
Witness the dance of peacocks
That wake the four corners of the world
And act as the chariot of God Kumaraswamy
Also, see the delicate dance of the cobra
          with diamonds on its head
I do not have time to narrate all the fantastic
          stories of Kailasa
Shiva wears a crescent moon on his head
And is the most romantic amongst all Gods
He will bless you on your journey

Be not deceived by the intoxicating smell of sandalwood
Those trees are home to the most poisonous snakes
If you are attracted to them
Death comes close
Sometimes danger tricks the mind and seduces
Do not stop there

In the eternal cycle of the universe
Skulls in the garland around Shiva's neck
Remind one of human mortality
They grin and mock death

The lovesick Chakora bird sips
On the overflowing milk of the full moon
The night has passed, go find your scraps of food
Oh queen of the bats, you are sage

In the wee hours, Budubukka arrived playing Dakka[63]
The sound of the Dakka breaks the eardrum
In the east, caste Hindus live
They claim to be decent people
But they don't tolerate friendship with us and become angry
Oh, saintly bird! The rooster is crowing
Go to the palace of the God Shiva

On your return journey, visit and make my fortune
Share what Lord Shiva told you
You live in temples and receive the grace of Gods
No one can be a better savior than you
It is already dawn in the East
Sunrays will steal the secrecy of our meeting
Go to your place as soon as possible

My house has no doors
You may enter anytime during the day or night
You do not need permission

Everyone is awake and are working on their spinning wheels
Tender sun rays are warming up the lap of Mother Earth

As though to meet the expectations of the untouchable
The Bat left for the temple of Shiva
As the landlord Sun hurried
The untouchable laborer tied his loincloth
And readied himself for work in the field

---

63 An hourglass-shaped musical drum played by Budubukkala men. They are a nomadic
community who perform devotional songs, ritual performances to heal diseased people,
and are also soothsayers. They go around villages, especially during the harvest season, to
collect grains and accept alms from people.

PREFACE TO PART II

It has been a while since Gabbilam went with the message to Kailasa. Our poor soul is waiting for her return. Because of this message to Kailasa, pleasant waves blew from four corners. Temple entry movement, Harijan upliftment, Gandhiji's spinning wheel made sounds of auspiciousness. India started getting rid of British colonialism. This untouchable (son of Arundhati) saw clouds carrying hopes that awakened him from despair. He forgot his timeless bonded slavery. Gabbilam came back to visit him. He welcomed her and asked whether her mission was a success or failure? From her mood, he understood it was a success. In these transcendent times, disputes among people of Andhra and India, selfishness, the dreadful disease of caste differences and religious hatred and indifference of the people added to the challenge of his liberation as counterproductive developments that anguished him. He started sharing his worries with his favorite goddess and symbol of his community, Gabbilam. She listened to him patiently. However, how can a bird, that does not have the strength or voice to speak, console him? She circumambulated with tears in her eyes and left to go to the temple of Shiva. His words without death continued to echo on the aerial route taken by Gabbilam and crystallized in the second part of the text. His efforts will be realized, if not today, tomorrow. One must wait to watch whether he is lucky enough to enjoy those fruits.

— Jashuva, 1946.

PART II

Meditation on Freedom

A son of our soil mesmerized everyone with his speech
At the World Parliament of Religions
By weaving a cotton thread
Won people of five continents
And Gandhi gained us independence
My fellow Telugu occupied the seat of a professorship
          at a Western university[64]
The world applauded our Bengali poet
For winning the Nobel Prize[65]
One of our compatriots found that even plants
          experience joy and sorrow[66]
But they never counted me as one of them
Always considered me an outsider
despite being their brother

---

64 Sarvepalli Radhakrishnan was a professor of Eastern Religions and Ethics at Oxford University during 1936–52.
65 Rabindranath Tagore was the first Indian and non-European to win the Nobel Prize in 1913.
66 Jagadish Chandra Bose was a pioneering botanist.

Not sure what the Bat told him
But the god Shiva had tears in his eyes
Stood up like a mountain
And vanished in seconds into dark clouds

When the doors of the Travancore temple
Opened its door for untouchables
Startled gods had to allow them to visit their temples
Offering untouchables solace for their miserable condition

The stain of untouchability
Made India lose its respectability in the comity of nations
There is no bigger weapon than forgiveness
To stop the war with Germany
Only a spinning wheel can win independence
Even if it takes three hundred years
Only the path of justice is the right way
The tears of untouchables crystallize into clouds
And burn the country like thunderstorms
Holding a stick and spinning wheel
The Gujarati Bania walked to the four corners of the country[67]

That message awakened the country
Along with the soiled coarse cloth
Malas and Madigas who live outside the village
                were recognized
And respected as human beings.

Brother Harijan! Do not be afraid
The chariot of independence is here[68]
You will have a place in it
Come along to pull it forward
Mother India welcomes you to join in her songs.

____

67 Refers to M.K. Gandhi's anti-untouchability campaign of 1932 as a protest against the separate electorates for Dalits. He also founded the Harijan Sevak Sangh.
68 Many Dalit intellectuals like Kusuma Dharmanna, Jala Rangaswamy and Nakka China Venkaiah used the metaphor of chariot to refer to 'self-rule.'

One day the ascetic Bat entered the house
Wandering freely with joyous flights
With excitement, he offered his gratitude
And asked did you convey my message?

Did you visit all those holy lands I described to you?
Did the great God and his wife host you?
Did they hear my words?
Did you see the golden rays?
Did the diamond-shaped snowflakes pierce through
          snowy caves and divine abodes?

Oh god, Shiva! Is it right to dance and entertain?
Sin in the world is spreading
Did you ask him to make one visit to our universe?

Oh, Bat! Did your message get praise like Kalidasa's *Meghaduta*?
The people of high-rank worship clouds and mountain peaks
My exceptional talents will not win praises because of
          my status as a slave

Did you come across the sages Vyasa and Valmiki?
Roaming in Kailasa, the heavenly abode
Once you notice their senectitude
You will understand the age of *Mahabharata* and *Ramayana*
Valmiki had profound compassion for animals and birds
This made him a great poet, and he wove a golden
          story of *Ramayana*
No one knows who taught the sacred Sanskrit
          to the thieving fisherman[69]
No education is impossible once God graces the ability

---

69 Sage Vyasa, considered to be the author of *Mahabharata*, was supposed to have been
born to a fisherwoman and sage Parashara. In reality, the Manusmriti prohibits education
for Shudras and untouchables and ascribing authorship to a man from the fishing commu-
nity is far-fetched and also an insidious way to keep the oppressed caste within the ambit of
Brahminism.

On your way, did you come across the romantic
                    cloud messenger of Kalidasa?
Its sounds and rapid movements shower pearls
One should not consider the message it carries
Just as a mythical story of fifteen years of separation between lovers
That story arouses even an older man to feel like a youth

As you carried an emotionally burdensome message of mine
How did you escape the raucous and destructive sounds of
                    the airplanes on your way?[70]
Alas, no peril can prevent the journey of a pilgrim by birth.

Did you enjoy the delightful sight of those snow mountains
                    resembling the divine bull?
They reach into the sky
With their shiny, sparkling white rays
Did you feel the luminescence as a blessed experience?

That silver mountain pierced like a hook
Into the hearts of the enemies of India as an unscalable barrier
It is a pearl garland to Mother India
That mountain curtailed the pride
Of the mountain among mountains, the caste mountain
For Shiva, who lives on this mountain
It is nature's wedding hall
Perennial rivers like the Ganga and Indus
Learned to walk here
Did you observe the footprints that cleanse sins and delight eyes?

Hunter, with bow and arrow, roamed in a dense forest
He strangled and flung people like animals
Those victims were oppressed classes

Great sculptors wondered
Amazed at dawn's color

---

70 The text was written during the World War II and refers to the sounds of warplanes.

Awakened from the silence of the night
Birds enjoyed twilight's glory
And wondered about the sculptor-creator who made
    those colorful skies
Also, ask about the village he came from?
Did you find out about him?
Are those creations not pleasurable?

Hesitant to exhibit their beauty
The celestial nymphs with lustrous eyes wander in clouds
Did you see them?
It seems they harvest pearls in deep oceans
And they are unimaginably fantastic creations

How many nightingale songs have been wasted
       in those darkened jungles?
Streams may have vanished in those heartless mountains
Bees disappeared, spraying fragrant perfumes
       on those dirty paths
Pearls might have scattered, falling on overgrown vegetation
Many sand creations, radiant gems, and nectar
Along with the peace they bring, they perished
       in the belly of nature
Their existence was wrecked because they were born
       in the wrong place
This is why so much injustice happened to them[71]

There is one old lady on the moon
She might be the disciple of Gandhi
And lives with her spinning wheel
God Shiva honoring her with the moon on his head
Dazzled by the moon, he rests in flower gardens
Does he listen to my message at all?

My mind only visualizes the image of my mother
After death, people say they live in Vaikunta or Kailasa
Did you see that land?
Here, no one knows about the afterlife

Both Sun and Moon move in the universe
But they envy one another
Why are they so hostile?
Who is Dravidian, and who is Telugu among them?[72]

---

71 Indirectly hinting at the wrongful birth of an untouchable in caste Hindu society.
72 This refers to the acrimony between Tamil and Telugu people in the Madras presidency.

Nature appears so fanciful during the day
Why does it get buried in mud in the darkness of the night?
Who is that villain, who humiliates it?
As the Sun goes down, he hides somewhere in the corner
Foolish people never feel ashamed of their acts
Instead, they persist in their wicked deeds

As they say, dancing Shiva never realized
          the eternal glory he had earned
And never felt the pride of his achievement
But nowadays, many performers become arrogant
          and ignore poets

True poets always search for precious ideas and meanings
Their imagination afloat in the sky on mountain tops
Did you hear their imagination while descending from
          those snowy mountains?
Only a finely tuned sensibility can discern it

By making his net with coarse cotton yarn
The hunter is trying to catch a lion called independence
Will he succeed, or will the lion escape the net?

Did you mention to Shiva that they do not touch
          their fellow human beings?
But worship a bull as Nandi and expect rewards in life
Did God Shiva become angry and show his prejudice?
And admonish untouchables?
Who are not supposed to possess the secrets
          of Vedic knowledge
And to ask questions?

By applying sacred ash to his forehead
Surrounded by wanton women
A great poet vows to control his carnal desires
Not even an enemy should face such a torturous trial

Some lead a selfish life
Devise new doctrines based on blind beliefs
And influence the minds of people

Some Telugus[73] return from foreign countries

Adopt foreign clothing and lifestyles
Their appearance is distasteful
 If they present themselves in elegant Telugu attire
One could praise them

From your facial expression
I understand there is no remarkable result from your mission
I made a mistake by troubling you so much
Our fate is to be wronged, so be it
For the sake of your beloved brothers
With courage, you faced God himself directly
It is a kind gesture, and we are immensely grateful

Failures are steppingstones to success
Do not agonize over it
Walls are built brick by brick
And result in a steady structure

I do not see it as my failure
And my efforts will never go to waste
Like a storm, my words will move God Shiva
          and his wife, Uma
If my heart-wrenching message fails
Winning independence with a spinning wheel
          will be empty

---

73 The author uses *Andhrulu* but this term can be used interchangeably for Telugu peo-
ple. Similar to Tamil, Bengali and Bihari communities, Telugus also migrated as indentured
laborers to Burma (now Myanmar), Mauritius, South Africa, the Caribbean and other Brit-
ish colonies in the nineteenth and early twentieth centuries.

At the beginning, full of compassion, Brahma Naidu
      laid the foundation of his kingdom[74]
Alas, it was destroyed later through false actions
In the end, do we not see the culture of compassion
      remembered as a success?
Similarly, Gandhi's efforts will not have been in vain

As gratitude for conveying my message
Kindly accept my tears as a holy bath
Other than that, do not expect much from me
If I get a place in the mansion of independence
Then I will pay you back

What share does each community get in independent India?
I might get a chance to rule
In our community's official flag
We will put your image as a symbol

Many great men can change our lives
Ameliorate our situation and bring us out of the dense
      darkness and suffering
Like a fool, I took shelter with a beggar Shiva
He does not have food to eat and clothes to wear
Thus, I failed to achieve what I desired

Oh, I forgot! Did you see the resident of Sabarmati Ashram?
Is that person equal to the supreme God and Buddha?
His laugh is as radiantly pure as moonlight
Bapuji does not care about white lords or even their superiors

---

74 The story of Brahma Naidu is associated with the anti-caste and anti-Brahminical movement. Thus, Jashuva's invocation of Brahma Naidu is part of an effort to associate his message with anti-caste histories. See Gene H. Roghair, *The Epic of Palnadu: A Study and Translation of Palnati Virula Katha, A Telugu Oral Tradition from Andhra Pradesh,* Clarendon Press, Oxford, 1982.

Amongst many, Vallabhbhai Patel can be counted
        as an equal to Gandhi
Did you have the good fortune to meet him?
He sacrificed all his wealth for the cause of independence
He understands our degradation

Jawaharlal Nehru has the iron will to rein in royal horses
He is a capable leader with education and maturity
Four corners of the world praise him
After independence, I hope he will not forget our plight

The tricolor Congress flag blooms charmingly like a hibiscus flower
It has many branches like a tree
And all communities get strength from it
Do we have a place to take shelter under its shade?

Our brother Ambedkar faced many hardships
Returned from Europe as an accomplished scholar
A giant among men and eligible for a viceroyship
Did he welcome and worship you with flowers?
Indeed! If he shows appreciation, this is the first step
        towards your victory

Unable to condemn the self-centered attitude of 'I and me'
The eighteen *Puranas* lost their sharpness
The vow of silence
Brought the sense of equality as 'I and you' signify togetherness

The English ruler's ministers arrived with
                a message to satisfy us
They come and go and help us willingly
In the same way, the crown of independence
                will arrive today or tomorrow
Like a pregnant woman who will not stop delivering a baby

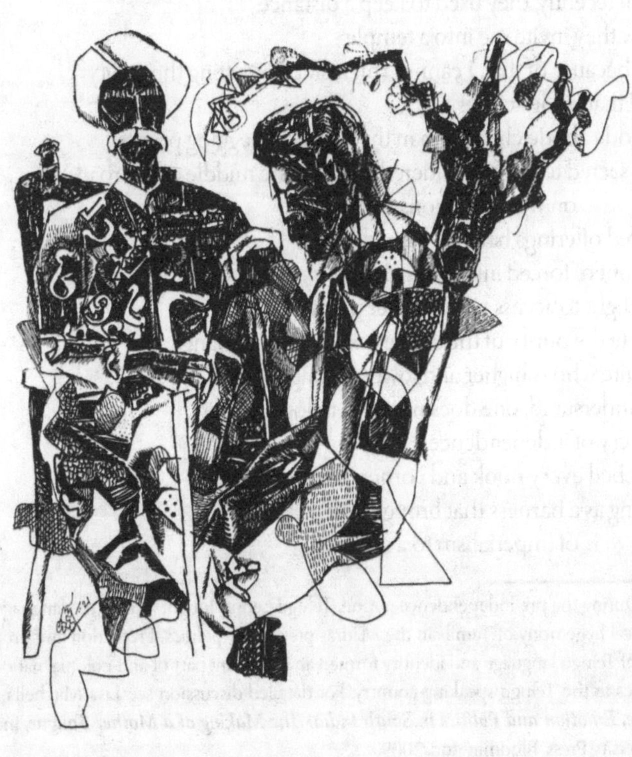

God in the temple sends messages with
         many asking me to visit him
Can I follow you? Should I come?
If the temple entry is delayed
There is a danger that people on a hunger strike will die
I will not bear the pain of a single death of an Andhra person[75]

Despite being a Bat
You were able to move God Shiva's world
To create waves in a still lake
One small stone is enough

Until recently, they used to keep a distance
Now they invite me into a temple
Just because of that, I cannot run inside, forgetting the reality
Will that bring self-respect?
Is God's abode cheaper than the streets of begging priests?
The sacred temple considered beneath the middle of the road
         on which millions walk?
Sacred offerings have become debased
In front of forced inter-caste dining
The fight to access village water tanks
Dilute the purity of the deepest waters of the Ganga
Inquire who is higher and lower among them
To understand, one does not have to look too far
The cry of independence
Reached every nook and corner of the world
Acting as a harness that brought the elephant
         of imperialism to a standstill[76]

---

75 During the pre-independence period, Telugu people fought against the language and political hegemony of Tamils in the Madras presidency politics. Protection and propagation of Telugu language and identity formed an important part of anti-colonial nationalist politics in the Telugu speaking country. For detailed discussion see Lisa Mitchell's *Language, Emotion and Politics in South India: The Making of a Mother Tongue*, Indiana University Press, Bloomington, 2009.

76 In brackets Jashuva says 'white people as elephants.'

Similarly, in the future, the same divine principle
            will restrain the tiger called untouchability
Announce to everyone that a promise has been made
            to address our demands
Today or tomorrow, it will come to fruition
Some might argue that it is impossible to accomplish
Comfort my friend by telling me which side you will stand

I am speaking many uncomfortable truths
By not winning your sympathy, I might get distressed
Or by bringing attention and compassion to honest persons,
            I might feel elated
Tell me, do not be afraid
See my teardrops expressed in these words

For the sake of renown, a poet might conceal his passion
            and compromise with the world
Might follow the path of worldliness like a mad man
That way, he will be a disgrace to the goddess of learning
A person without conscientiousness will become an adopted
            child of a rich man

Your deeds might result in the birth of a great poet in our community
Despite his accomplishments and outstanding artistic
            and literary talent
He will not be eligible for great fame
In this fallen country that obsessively argues about high
            and low birth
What can be more pathetic than this?

Our charitable deeds are strange
Vemana[77] wrote exceptional poetry with twisted sarcasm

---

77 Yogi Vemana was a non-Brahmin, early modern, anti-caste rationalist poet. He wrote against caste, Brahminical rituals and practices using a tinge of sarcasm and common sense. Charles Philip Brown, the compiler of the first Telugu to English dictionary, collected and translated the verses of Vemana. *Vemana Padyamulu (The Verses of Vemana: Moral, Religious and Satirical)*, Madras, 1911.

That had the power to make dense forests chuckle
        and sprout more
Still, no one gave a fistful of rice when he was alive
Now they leave garlands and perform rituals at his tomb

After death, he was christened Saibaba
When alive, he was a worthless Sayibaiah[78]
This is the essence of life and death
Even the God at Tirupati will not know the inner meaning

I have had to describe strange and painful things
About impartiality, affection
It just slipped my tongue to talk
About norms, laws and baseless slippery bonds
Virtues, kindness, and crocodile tears

Today by displaying a rock as being the God Eshwara
Kotappa, an ordinary family man, amasses wealth
By collecting bribes in God's name
If stone rubble can become gods
Why cannot they swallow heaps of wealth?
Oh, bird! There is no hope for my starving
        brethren in this situation

Vemana wrote timeless poetry
He was chief amongst his Reddy caste
His genius went unacknowledged by the expert chronicler
        of Telugu literature[79]
Being counter to the dominant culture, Vemana was abandoned
And excluded from the history of Telugu poets

---

78 Muslims in Andhra Pradesh were referred to as Sayibulu. Even though the term sounds benign, it carries an invisible derogatory meaning. Shiridi Saibaba, who is worshipped across Telugu- speaking regions as a saint, hailed from the Muslim community.

79 Kandukuri Veeresalingam was a pioneering social reformer and the modernizer of Telugu literature. He wrote *Andhra Kavula Charitram* (Chronicle of Telugu Poets) in three parts. In this work, non-Brahmin anti-caste thinkers were not included. Jashuva, as an anti-caste thinker, pointed out these omissions.

Some write poetry using bombastic words
These are equal to big rocks, which scare people
            when they roll
It is meant only for pundits
Like a divine cow that serves the gods exclusively
Their poetry never reaches ordinary folks

A premature baby can be made strong and healthy
When fed a nutritious diet
Similarly, a poet will be applauded for a powerful theme
Even when the length of the poem is short

Grammarians obsessed with technicalities
Complain about appropriate use of syntax
Not appreciating the organization
And the aesthetic elegance of the poetic creation

Many exquisite words are not in use
Some become obsessed with ancient poetry
And linguistic refinements
The ocean of rural folklore contains tasteful Telugu words[80]
We are not learning their secrets and meanings

Did you discover the way Krishna Devaraya led
            the chariot of wisdom?
That consisted of eight court poets as *Ashtadiggajas*[81]
Telugus have forgotten that
In those noxious ruined caves and hills
Melodies of poetic creations
Languish in insignificance

---

80 Jashuva brought the words used by the unlettered village folks into the classical Telugu literary idiom. In this way he stood out as the most creative Telugu poet, whose poems were sung by villagers to stage dramas with ease, and which resonated with their own lived experiences.

81 *Ashtadiggajas* were eight court poets of Krishna Devaraya, the ruler of the Vijyanagara empire.

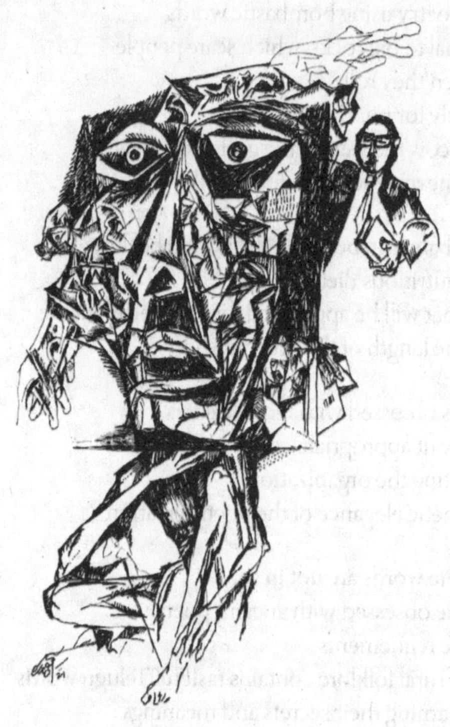

The exuberance of Telugu threatened its enemies
The Telugu sculptors' hammer-beats reached China
As giant Telugu poets roared
The Telugu flag reached the four corners
Raised in the streets of Vijayanagara[82]
People burst into laughter at the thought
            of Tenali Ramalinga[83]
Did you see the beautiful happiness dance
            in those ruined forts?

---

82 The Vijayanagara kingdom is celebrated as the apex of Telugu literary and cultural re-surgence.

83 Tenali Ramakrisha, also known as Tenali Ramalinga, was one of the *ashtadiggajas* in the court of Krishna Devaraya. He was renowned for his wit.

At the battle of Talikota[84]
When the Muslim warriors surrounded and pressed
The courageous Telugu ruler lost his land
Those sly gods and goddesses
Whom he worshipped, offered favors and prayers for ages
It is laughable that none of them came to his rescue

Even at the age of ninety, the Rama Raya was
          a mighty king like Bhima
He married an audacious ruler's daughter[85]
It is inconceivable to Telugus that he brought troubles
          upon himself
By provoking Muslims to unite against him
That humiliation haunts us always

The Vijayanagara city is Telugu London
A Telugu citadel
It was a seat of great Telugu poets
A poet was honored and paraded on an elephant[86]
Because of the arrogance of Aliya Ramaraya[87]
The citadel was broken into pieces

---

84 In the battle of Talikota, the Deccani Sultanates defeated the last Vijayanagara ruler, Aliya Ramaraya on January 23, 1565. It was a final blow to the empire and led to its eclipse in history. For details see Robert Sewell, *A Forgotten Empire: A Contribution to the History of India*, London, S. Sonnenschein & Company, 1900 and Burton Stein, *The New Cambridge History of India: Vijayanagara*, Cambridge, Cambridge University Press, 2005.

85 Krishna Devaraya's daughter.

86 This refers to Allasani Peddana, one of the court poets of the emperor Krishna Devaraya. The emperor personally placed *gandapendaramu* (golden ring) around the right ankle of Peddana as a sign of distinction as a poet and paraded him on an elephant in the streets of Vijayanagara.

87 Aliya Ramaraya was the son-in-law of Krishna Devaraya and de facto ruler of Vijayanagara; the empire's glory ended under his rule.

If the secrets at home were not revealed
And our people did not collude with others
I would have pounded mountains into dust
And crushed the hearts of our enemies
Walked proudly with head held high in the assembly of emperors
Like rocks splash bubbles
I would have recited lustrous poems of hope and radiance
Decorated the chignon of a Telugu lady with the garland of glory
And raised the Telugu flag on the highest peak of the
          Himalayas as the symbol of victory

The pedestal of knowledge sat on the island with gemstones
          scattered everywhere
Those were our treasury of swords
That is the radiance of the Telugu ruler's achievement
It was only for Telugu warriors to display the way people
          lived in happiness

Many places exhibit Telugu arts and culture
Numerous stories scared enemies to death
Until today we retain the brave stripes of Palnadu on our bodies
We do not mingle with others
That is our disadvantage

There is blazing unity amongst Muslim warriors
And the brave Muslim soldiers guard their house with tenacity
The *sambar*[88] loudly announces
That the Dravidians are busy making money
The Hindi language is spreading to different regions
And becoming a lingua franca
Strange are the times
Hindi is emerging as a national language like a flower on the head
The rich Telugu lady used to apply
Blood-like vermillion to the forehead with ferocity
Never distressed

---

88 *Sambar* (mixed lentil and curry/vegetable soup) is a staple dish of South India that is associated with Dravidians.

The precious treasure that used to adorn
            the river Gautami Ganga
Plundered by the Muslim rulers
Treasures of our forefathers
Will never be retrieved even if they come alive
My land,[89] once lit by gemstones, now pleads
            for a drop of oil

When thieves stole our jewels
When enemy kings cleverly seized the wealth
            of bravery with sweet talk
Did not the Goddess Durga, in her avatar as Chandi,
            display her power with a million hands?
Or did she lose courage and embrace hatred towards
            other religions?[90]

What is the use in boasting?
Will the parents of God Krishna rise from their graves?
The fearless Telugu heroes used to rage like a fire
There are many brethren eager to awaken those in slumber

The day when our poets' tongues can speak a universal truth
The day they point out problems in perception and
            show the right path
The day their minds are not influenced by fabricated stories
The day our education's brightness does not let our iron-willed
            society rust
The day words will not let one become lazy, hide their
            talent, and beg
For that auspicious day, my broken heart longs and prays

---

89 He uses 'rashtra' here.
90 This refers to the Hindu-Muslim riots in Bengal in the 1940s that resulted in the dis-
placement and killing of thousands of people.

They spent years describing the marriages of rulers
And exposed dazzling residences of queens
With the seductive depiction of pangs of separation
With salacious tales of addicted youths that ruined their futures
Annoyed by the repeated recitation of Rama's fables
They ignored the sufferings of grieving refugees[91]
Instead of using the art of poetry for the benefit of humanity
They plunged it into the ocean of selfishness

Like aged bodies
The stacks of scriptures that won't teach us wisdom become
                part of our education
Even after ten thousand years
The obdurate will be born
They live by serving selfish people
What is the use of telling many uninspiring stories that
                will not awaken?

They believe that without the presence of a woman in the text
It will not attain the status of a masterpiece
Some poets with an eye on money
Sing second rate poems with love epithets
And entertain the ruling classes
Instead, today's poets must write compassionately

The goddess of famine is the daughter of the recent War
In the streets of the rich, who eat sumptuous food
Can the painful cries, starved bellies and exposed bones
                of the destitute be visible?
The learned poet, Tagore's pen[92]
Cannot comprehend the anguish of the new poetry

---

91 Buddha talks about the importance of feeding the hungry instead of preaching to them about ethics. Jashuva borrows from multiple anti-caste traditions in this context.

92 The poet Rabindranath Tagore is referred as *Kavindrudu* in Telugu and Jashuva points out that Tagore's elitist background prevents him from comprehending the anguish of a new Dalit poet like himself.

There are many pacifists in our country
They hesitate to kill ants
And get statues of Buddha carved by breaking stones
Compassion became scarce in Bengal
Were there no caring people?
Were the rich not eating sumptuous meals?[93]

How did the tradition that believed in non-permanence die?
Why do we have meaningless laws and standards written
                on palm leaves?[94]
The land that gave birth to the tradition
That refused to avenge even physical attacks

And moved the hearts of enemies
Why are the snakes of unrest hissing everywhere?
The writings of ascetic Vivekanand written with his tears
                that have not dried

Which great soul will bring victory to my country and unfold
                like a golden pasture?
Condemn old and ignorant traditions, and spread education
                like alms

Lank bodies that can be swept away in the wind
Wearing saffron shawls and empty pumpkin shells around their hips
Corrupted in every aspect of life, roam as ascetics, addicted to cannabis
Oh, ascetic bird! Did you come across them?

Meditating or reciting prayers
There are many in villages dressed as monks who wander
                around cheating people
Teaching false doctrines to fulfill desires
To exploit women, they wear the mask of devotion

---

93 In reference to the Bengal famine of 1943.

94 In the premodern period, ancient and medieval texts were written mostly on palm leaves. Metal plates and rock edicts were other forms of enacting laws, declaring jurisdiction and sending messages.

Milk, fruits, and root vegetables are the only foods we eat
I can never desire anything else
A little bit of gold or silver is enough as a gift
Gosais[95] employ tricks and frauds
They are ruling the roost across the country
All crafts rusted; begging has become a prominent profession
          in multiple forms
In such a situation, how can we not have famines?
Many have the ambition to improve the country
But no one would like to wipe out this scourge and bring good
          fortune to the country

Many fertile lands have become shallow fields
With thorny shrubs, turned into barren lands
Beggars eat and digest
And their strength gets wasted

Some parasites occupy positions of power
Every day they demand bribes and milk people
Poor laborers buy gifts for them with their hard-earned money
Did you come across such bizarre impersonators and their devotees?
Oh, mother bird! Never beg from them

They maltreat fellow humans and worship the God Narayana
The earth is full of wicked people
Being unable to put feet on it
You move upside down, facing the sky

---

95 Historically Gosai vagabonds played an important role in trade and mobilized people
against oppressive regimes using indigenous tools and networks. For example, see Bernard
Cohn, 'The Role of the Gosains in the Economy of Eighteenth and Nineteenth-Century
Upper India,' *Indian Economic and Social History Review*, Vol. 1, No. 4, 1964, pp. 175–82.
   Dirk Kolff, 'Sanyasi Trader-Soldiers,' *Indian Economic and Social History Review*,
Vol. 8, 1971, pp. 213–20.

A priest guards the treasure box
And serves secondary gods
Organizes celebrations for bloodthirsty gods
Carries chariots at the yearly marriage celebrations of artificial Rama
I also climbed the temple steps of the hill god Venkateshwara
And he robs people and tonsures their heads?
I also poured money into the river goddess Ganga
In the name of *Pushkara*[96] took a dip
In the middle of the stream
By cleansing so many sins
I am left with just a loincloth

The crazy era of flying horses was over long ago
This is an era of science and Gandhian intelligence
With swords and sticks, you cannot rule people

The quagmire of caste difference has existed for ages
It enslaved and kept people in poverty
These are the days to overcome this and progress further
Provide shelter to farmers
Crushed under the wheels of the king's chariot
Understanding that differences amongst humans, as being
   high and low, is a blot
Protect people victimized in the name of religious traditions
   and practices
One should also realize that the mother tongue is more
   delightful than the official language[97]

---

96 *Pushkaralu* is marked every twelve years in celebration of twelve sacred river goddess-
es. People take a dip in large numbers in celebration of the occasion.

97 In the context of colonial English, many poets across language traditions resisted the
hegemonic power of English and realized the strength of the mother tongue to express
emotions. Raja Rao in a foreword to his famous novel *Kanthapura* (1938) writes 'The
tempo of Indian life must be infused into our English expression, even as the tempo of
American or Irish life has gone into the making of theirs. We in India, think quickly, we talk
quickly, when we move, we move quickly' and makes a fundamental distinction between
the story telling tradition of India and that of English.

There are many fraudulent nationalists in Kailasa
They wear *khaddar* in winter
And say we will get independence
The cry of great men for the betterment of untouchables
Comes with bittersweet tears

Our wretched community suffers from the disease of not
        wishing to cause pain to anyone
For this, I do not have to feel miserable about myself
I bothered you out of eccentricity
Oh, bird! The person with self-esteem
Should not be born into the most distressed community of all

Oh mother, let me tell you one thing
In the farmland of India
The disease of untouchability afflicted Malas and Madigas also
Not just God Shiva and Krishna
Even those who reject Krishna, the Christians
I feel ashamed to say that even they failed to unite them[98]

I served the Telugu community like a slave for fifty years
Neither happiness nor comfort ever touched the threshold
        of my house
I must wait the rest of my life with buried expectations
Even God Shiva will not tell whether they will perish or be fulfilled

I am unsure whether the birth of mother earth's child
Will be auspicious or not
Childbirth is an enormous burden to the mother

Revolutionaries and rationalists deliver grand speeches
        about compassion
All this is bogus
When people butcher howling animals and tear their stomachs
Dance foolishly and celebrate in the flowing river of blood
They watch and show others and encourage them

---

98 Jashuva wrote eloquently about the caste differences in Christianity and as a result lost his
job as a teacher. In the Indian subcontinent, caste differences and hierarchy exist in all religions.

Kunti gave birth to Karna and abandoned him in the river Ganga
His handsome physique, talents wasted, she cried with grief
Similarly, the Kunti mother of India gave birth to countless Karnas
Oh, saintly bird! Even now, the Pandavas do not recognize
        our kinship[99]

One ties the garland of *rudraksha* to his head[100]
Epitomizes himself as God Shiva
Another emerges with upright marks on the forehead
        and abhors Shiva Linga[101]
One more is different from the other two and wears
        strange costumes
He challenges both
Someone else enslaved to marijuana applies ash all over the body
And appears in a guru avatar
One more bounces up and down, claiming
Oh, human being! Ours is a heavenly religion
If many religions fight with each other like this
Where is the way for unity?

---

99 Jashuva uses the oppressed and marginalized characters in *Mahabharata* to draw a parallel with the existential condition of Dalits. Karna in *Mahabharata* is a fascinating character, his birth to unwed Kunti, abandonment and his talent as an unrivalled archer/ warrior and the loyalty he displays are exemplary. But belonging to a marginalized community he never got what he deserved as a talented archer and warrior. He remains an anti-hero and victim of cunning Brahaminical caste patriarchical power play like many Dalits in history. Karna was born to the same mother as the Pandavas, but he never got the same recognition and treatment. Similarly, Dalits are never treated as fellow human beings by caste Hindu society.

100 *Rudraksha* (tear drops of Shiva who is known as Rudra) are dried seeds of a Elaeocarpus Ganitrus tree and are used as prayer beads by Shaivites.

101 Historically, phallic worship was popularized by Lingayats in medieval South India who worshipped Shiva. Lingayat monks, known as Jangamas, instructed their adherents to wear the Shiva Linga as a symbol of social equality. For a fascinating history of phallic worship in human history see Hargrave Jennings, *Phallic Miscellanies: Facts and Phases of Ancient and Modern Sex Worship, as Illustrated Chiefly in the Religions of India* (https://www.gutenberg.org/files/36254/36254-h/36254-h.htm).

On the pretext of vows, the toddler is thrown into the Ganga
In the name of the custom of Sati
Many young wives are sacrificed to God Agni and burned to ashes
The evil tradition that confined education to the few
Nipped the talents and aspirations of many to pursue knowledge
We lost collective strength by living separately from each other
By making statues and installing them
Spent ages worshipping Buddha, Jesus, and Gandhi
Only through education can we eradicate that stupidity
Unable to feed the cold-blooded rock-hearted spirits day and night
Incapable of giving gifts to gurus
As part of the inescapable custom, we face harassment
Trapped by the lazy sorcerers and their black magic
We lost confidence
Unable to bear the lion-like roars of innumerable cruel religions
Being jealous of one's own brothers' wealth
Helpless to get rid of the attachment
To foolish rituals
Praised by the gods, my country's progress
Suspended between heaven and emptiness[102]

Oh, hermit bird! I am not qualified to organize a feast
Nor to invite you to eat as a guest
In this useless society, there are thirty thousand castes
By worshiping cobras, my country becomes a laughingstock

As a revered bird, you sit and eat along with God Shiva
You eat food cooked by the goddess of harvest[103] for her husband
Yours is a blessed clan
As a saintly bird
Will you follow caste differences and refuse an invitation
             from a destitute friend?

---

102 In Telugu *uttiki* means a sling in which cooked food is hung. In the context of heaven,
it is appropriate to replace sling with emptiness.
103 Goddess Annapurna is associated with food and nourishment.

My caste kin are writing with their blood
Exceptional poetry in support of a genre of compassion
Will they melt the diamond-hard hearts of greed?
Will our wishes be cut short like pollen that failed
          to germinate a seed?

He hails the poet to his face
Behind his back, terms it a blemish on the art
He becomes enthralled listening to poetry
Knows I have no caste
Donates thousands of rupees to members of his caste
Sends others on their way with flattery
With contempt for the sculptor
Worships the statues made by him
In such a country with its wicked people
Of course, the arts will be dead

Can Shakespeare, Byron and Goldsmith compete with our
          Timmanna and Tikkana?
Today, there is disgust for our poets and language
Foreign language poets enchant us
All this is because our age is being magically influenced
          by foreign literature
The fight for independence is like a war
And enthusiasm for it stimulates and awakens the four
          caste communities
Shall we get a share in the comfortable paradise called independence
Oh, sister, tell me! Will they say we have no part and turn us away?

Andhra brothers agitated for a separate Telugu state
Sounds of their unrest echoes in the caves of Mount Meru
You might feel glad that they will succeed
All their rage is like the frenzy of a fizzy drink

Holy Jesus sacrificed himself for the welfare of humanity
For the celebration of universal happiness, different religions, diverse sects
Teachings about nothingness and *Veda*s show the means of liberation
Their essence captured like pearls in the palm of a hand

In a place where the poor will not feel distressed
Looking at rich people's food
In a society where customs will not roar like a lion and scare others
And let knowledge flourish
Where the arts are not trampled
Under the feet of the demon of communal or caste hatred
Where freedom and liberty
Can stand up to the brutal knives of the ruler
Did you see such a place?
Where orphans are loved and kissed as if it were their own parents
Tell me, and there I would like to live

Nothing is more immoral than an outward display of deceptive smiles
Polite talk and fake relationships
And enmity afterwards
Is there a civilization in which such wicked Satans do not roam on earth?
Even if there is one foot of land
Kindly let me know, there I will build my house

A country that practises the cruel culture of suppressing the arts
Has no liberty
Is there a way for civility in the world?
They justify caste in ninety ways with irrelevant answers
We come across people who deceive and kill the arts in this holy land

There are many secrets hidden in this precious body
It works like a machine that fears life
If its operational mechanism breaks down
No knowledge can repair it
Why did the mechanic hide secrets?
No one knows

Scientists have invented marvelous machines
But have died without discovering the roots of life and death
Even the gods who said they knew have also died
God who did not surrender the power to triumph over death
Where is he hiding? That cruel God
Why is he deceiving us?

Corpses of our ancestors have turned into manure
It has enabled the earth goddess to grow varieties
         of plants and fruits
Blessed humans to live in happiness
Their blood met clouds
And delights with rains
Every living being that dies comes back in some other form

Bodies of the dead rot for ages in the earth
After undergoing chemical metamorphosis
They transform into the bodies of babies
Otherwise, from where will their divine radiance come?

Because of penance, that birth will attain divine status
And you have learned the techniques of many rituals
Your ancestors and their goddesses suffered social and caste exclusion
Did the gods settle the issue?
The screams of the destitute will always be unbearable

Where there is a place in which universities respect the mother tongue
No pain is caused to the people, and they are not crushed
         and eaten every day
The soft-spoken words of the poets are expressed freely
Where parents do not teach their children about high
         and low caste differences
Where there are no traces of the venomous smiles
         of cunning people
Your abode is the shelter for the destitute who have no place
         or companion

We did not have exemplary writings
That would inspire us from childhood
With a flame of national consciousness
We did not have a mother-goddess-like Jijabai[104]
Who would raise us with discipline and bravery?
We did not have gods who could make everyone wear
Similar clothes and follow the same traditions
We lacked a ruler who could unite and protect people
When they were ready to turn against each other along caste lines
In pursuit of power and prestige
That has a momentary existence like a bubble
Unable to trust and make others trust
The lives of our nation shattered

Even now, preachers raise so many hopes
And tell us that a savior will come and sit on a throne
                    in the sky
And it is a truth
Try to prove stories from the ancient past
I do not want a paradise
That curtails my bravery, passion, and anger
One that enslaves me permanently

Even before I was born, my mind was killed
Religion killed my natural abilities
Which preacher will free me from these shackles?
I cannot even climb up to catch a sling hanging from the beam[105]
They promise to take me to paradise to swing in a cradle
Should I believe?

---

104 Jijabai was a hero of the 1857 war against British rule, which was the first war fought for India's independence.

105 In Telugu, the term *uttikekkaleni* addresses two situations: Jashuva's social position being at the bottom, he is unable to attain even a midway point in the hierarchy. Second, symbolically, the sling on which the cooked vessel is stored hangs from a beam. The protagonist does not even have a sling in his house.

Will the God who created me, will He be born again after me?
Because I cannot raise my voice
His thousand avatars make me anxious
Does he require golden arches for temples as gifts?
Will he accept the deceitful plots of his devotees?

The sacred texts which cannot change their words
What will they teach other than selfishness?
A god on the mountain respects me based on caste
Will he try to wipe away my tears?
A society addicted to mental slavery
Will it ever forge a friendship with me?
By telling unnatural stories
It imagines truth
The warm blood in the veins of our people has dried up
And they surrender and bow
Will they digest heroic tales and overwhelm their enemies?

The God Vishnu, the father of Brahma, said
He will be born to establish *dharma*[106]
Even today, I do not see him appearing above our head
We lose nothing even if he is not born at all

---

106 In Hinduism *dharma* refers to Sanatan Dharma that believes in a caste-based patriarchal social order. In *Mahabharata*, Krishna which is another form of Vishnu, tells Arjuna that he will be reborn at the end of every epoch to restore *dharma*:

Paritranaya sadhunam
Vinasaya ca duskrtam
Dharma-samsthapanarthaya
Sambhavami yuge yuge

Everything is sacred in this country
Nothing is more monstrous than caste
You will not see an animal lower than an untouchable
When my rights were robbed
Humanity turned into animality and aggression
Religion is a cruel animal like a lion grinding its teeth
To jealousy to suppress my anger
With deceitful teachings
Oppresses me

The world applauds, and they feel proud for earning
    B.A. and M.A. degrees
Our Malas and Madigas add fire to the subcaste fights[107]
Instead of bringing them together
They live within the limits of caste
There is no use in teaching such a depraved community

There is a saying, 'Already she has no nose; on top of it,
    she has a severe cold.'
Our caste slaves fight among themselves
They cannot differentiate good from the bad
I feel ashamed of these weak people
Gandhi recites the horrors of untouchability
Unaware of these internal fights

---

107 Jashuva is self-critical in reflecting on the issue of the practice of caste difference and prejudices among Dalits. The Mala-Madiga differences, in Telugu states, not only divided Dalits vertically but also led to separate political outfits that contributed to the further marginalization and rise of violence against Dalits. For critical reflection on the history of Mala-Madiga differences see Chinnaiah Jangam, 'Subcaste Consciousness and Challenges before Dalit Intellectuals,' *Mainstream*, March 19, 1997, pp. 21–25 and Sambaiah Gundimeda, 'Social Justice and the Question of Categorization of Scheduled Caste Reservations: The Dandora Debate in Andhra Pradesh' in Ramnarayan Rawat and K. Satyanarayana (eds), *Dalit Studies*, Duke University Press, 2016, pp. 202–32,

Provided, there are innocent people
Who prostrate themselves in fear upon hearing unnatural
        stories, *Vedas* and sacred texts
There will be poets who will swim in the ocean of luxuries
Will such a literary world give birth to a poet who acts like
        a dawn's light?

Like actors, we become loyal
To the religious laws that have evolved throughout history
Throw the society into a prickly bush
Continue domination over the poor
In that case, even the lies will become truths out of indifference

They averted the growth of Karna in war
By burying his power
But now his story is spread like a light everywhere
Similarly, sometimes with spite and jealousy,
        one can hide some power
It will erupt and raise its flag in another time

To protect the honor of Arjuna
God Krishna said so many things
Everyone is aware of that
It is laughable to imagine that Arjun can win against Karna

Even when I refuse to accept
Gods and their theories haunt and imprison me
My natural abilities and energy froze in dense cowardice
Oh, saintly bird! A Bat like you can teach thousands of lessons
But all these will become food for the wind

Did you see any weapons that can kill the flames
        of jealousy?
Did you see Vedic schools that teach tolerance
        of other religions?
Did you see any country ruled peacefully which has
        the disease of caste?
Did you come across places where a human will bounce
        like a fish upon seeing fellow human beings?
I get exhausted by beating drums and dancing[108]
Assuage the goddess of *shakti*[109]
Fruits of these efforts will be distributed among others
Did you come across such a vile land?

Cruel and abhorrent people stole my rights
They drove me from the village
Now they are trying to appease us
Many organizations are building tiny houses
Using them to amass wealth for themselves
Our people do not trust them

As the blood in their veins evaporates
They work hard to carve rock into sculptures
Because of parochial and contaminated writings
They are never acclaimed for their talents
Envious tongues can never utter truths
Some even doubt God's decisions as well

What is the power of knowledge?
That cannot eradicate the practice that tramples people
Is education a tasteful food for a tiger called stupidity?
Does it act as a guard for deceptive writings?
An education that does not foster humanity
Is like ecstasy from drugs

---

108 Traditionally, Madigas are drummers and Jashuva hails from that caste from his mother's side.
109 Refers to divine power.

In this country, for ages, different religions and communities lived
I do not believe that there will be peace and stability
Oh, bird! Can Muslims and Hindus drive the chariot
          of independence together?
Can the elephants of the South and North graze together?

They say a great God will be born
He will slay wicked men and roar with righteousness
          with a thousand faces
Sowing fear in my weak heart
This false message is the reason for insanity and blind beliefs

Which holy man let me be born into this unkind world?
In the same way, they lit the fire of hunger in my stomach
          without any smoke
Somehow, I endure the suffering
To eat the food, I found
Gods are taking shape as trees, anthills, and many other avatars

As he lamented his painful suffering
She expressed sympathy with warm tears in her eyes
After circumambulating, she left for her own house
          to eat offerings to God
Precisely at that time in the East
In a cradle, independent India popped out in the form of a toddler sun

With the saintly bird's coming and going
The poor man's blood has been drained
Because of this, he might die
If alive, he might even taste death

ABOUT THE TRANSLATOR

Chinnaiah Jangam was born in Telangana, southern India, and has attended the University of Hyderabad, Jawaharlal Nehru University (JNU) and School of Oriental and African Studies (SOAS), University of London. He is now an Associate Professor in the Department of History at Carleton University in Ottawa, Canada. He has held a postdoctoral fellowship at the International Center for Advanced Studies, New York University and has received the Harry Frank Guggenheim Foundation Dissertation Fellowship and the Felix Scholarship. He has taught at Osmania University in Hyderabad and Wagner College in New York City. He is the author of *Dalits and the Making of Modern India*, 2017 which was published in Telugu by Hyderabad Book Trust, 2020. He has contributed articles to books, journals, magazines and newspapers, online and in print, in Telugu and English. He also translates poetry and songs from Telugu to English.